How To Love Each Other Better

How To Love Each Other Better

James A. Vick

JAV Publishing
2019

First Printing: 2019

ISBN 978-0-359-84785-3

JAV Publishing
Fredericksburg, VA 22407

Ordering Information:

Special discounts are available on quantity purchases by corporations, associations, educators, and others. For details, contact JAV Publishing at 704-221-8524.

Contents

Acknowledgements

I would like to thank all the people who kept praying for me. My family, specifically my mother, who has instilled a lot of great meaning motivation, stories, and focus. All which has laid the foundation of everything that I know and been in my life, I love you always.

To my father who I have watched over the years. You may not have been perfect, but your presence in the home was very important for my development. By seeing you work and provide for our family, I witnessed the silence in your eyes with just a look placed the fear of God in me along with me learning respect and discipline. I appreciate you.

To my loving sister where would I be with you in my life. I can never give you enough credit for what you have done and meant to me as a child growing up and as a grown man.

To my brothers I have learned to watch and grow from each one of you. By being the youngest of the group, the life lessons I've learned of how to cultivate my own voice, knowing the proper time to use my lessons and voice with purpose.

To my other set of brothers, I love you all and thank you. Thank you for all the good times, laughs, talking trash sessions from a distance, to witnessing everybody growing up and developing into their own man. We always seem to connect back together and realistically never losing the connections not as friends, but brothers. I appreciate you

To my princess who has my heart and I really learned the meaning of what loves is from a little girl who looks like me has my mannerism and my joking personality I love you so much Aniyah M. Vick. I thank God for you every day that I was blessed to have you come into my life.

To all my sideline haters and complainers, I love you and you have a special place in my heart of not mattering at all. I utilize you to push me and I'm so thankful for God along this journey he never allowed me to become lame. Thank you so much sideline complainer you were needed.

Preface

I have been in prayer and meditation for quite some time. I thought about what I could say and do to uplift people more while they are going through their own life journeys. I am a man of observation. By working in the human service industries, I have been able to have numerous different interactions with people and families. Society has changed the mission of the way we love each other and the perception of men.

Men have no respect for themselves, women who they are supposed to love and protect, or the children they are supposed to teach and lead. Through my observations, the lines have been blurred. Please don't get me wrong, change is good but there is a price. There are more opportunities, but somewhere along this journey of life, we have hit a brick wall.

The question is, where do we go from this point? How do we love each other better? Is it possible to change how we love, admire, respect, listen, and be present in other's lives? Or is it now just a lost cause or battle not even suiting up for? Respect has been lost and values have become played out to some.

Introduction

As you realize how broken you are on the inside, you will start to see how much you are dying too. If you do not try to heal, depression and other thoughts will set in. People will create their own narrative about you. They will find ways to bring up your past just to throw it in your face to not support you. People who attempt to tarnish your name or reputation DO NOT LOVE YOU; it just shows different levels of self-hate. You may walk alone as you discover self-love and loving others better. But you are not alone, the higher power is guiding you. Let me enlighten you, shopping, drugs, sex, working out, group functions, activities, trips and being in denial will only work for so long. Being numb to life is real. Don't destroy yourself and others because you are healing or numb. The ultimate journey is to become wealthy in your soul, spirit, and to discover a level of people you never knew existed before.

Chapter 1

The Start of the Promise

I have been asked several times why you call yourself The Ambassador, for me I have always felt and thought there were some powerful things I was supposed to be and should be doing with my life. My life has been based on being a servant to other individuals by helping, guiding, teaching, counseling along with loving and showing guidance to other people to push them closer to their dreams and goals. So even with those jobs of my past, I have been led to do them they were always about other people. Truly I have had some dirty jobs, but those jobs helped build character and learning how to appreciate things more and people that were placed in my path for me to help them and for me to learn from them. But as an Ambassador, my job is to bring peace to several different situations and change the mindsets of others. The goal is to get individuals and groups of people to think differently. Truly my job is to honor my father's name and be of good courage.

I was reading a book by Max Lucado entitled It's Not About Me, which is a great book I might add. But at the end of the book Max was discussing a story he was having with a Rabbi and stated what Paul wrote: We are ambassadors for Christ, as though God were making an appeal through us (2 Corinthians 5:20). The ambassador has a singular aim to represent the King's reputation and present the King's will. The ambassador elevates the name of the King. So that's what I stand on and that is what I strive to do and be daily. The starting place of my promise is to push and motivate others by any means necessary. Often it does not look or feel good, but the core purpose of an ambassador is to bring peace and different perspectives in your heart and mind.

When I decided to look back over my life, I was able to see a lot of the things I have done and helped facilitate a lot of trouble that led to a road of pain and destruction. One of the most important principles was not obeying God's plan and order for my life. God has a plan for each individual and as human beings we choose often to do things our own way or the way a situation feels for the time being. Which typically can and will lead to a long road of heartache and pain when you don't follow the plan and path that God has tailored for you. God gives us free will and he does not force us to do anything. Now God does give us warning signs and prevision on a lot of our choices and decisions, we tend to choose and decide on. So, while the journey is not comfortable God still has his hands on you. He will bring things back into proper perspective and divine order where it was supposed to be for your own individual promise.

As I reflect and look over my life I noticed other character flaws within myself from playing games, not allowing other individuals to get close to me, not being completely open and honest, not lying just withholding some of the truth or pretty much telling you what I wanted you to know which is nothing. I am not an open book and there are certain things you are not supposed to know until I feel comfortable with you to express those things to you. Basically, things are expressed on a need to know basis. I personalized and internalized those thoughts. In my mind, I thought you should ask the appropriate questions and you would get the right information and a half answer. People have told me withholding information is the same as lying. You are a liar!!! Withholding information that will hurt or damage a person is not a mature way to handle a situation. As a mature adult, you should give other people the opportunity to see if they want to be bothered or deal with you. Therefore, withholding powerful information is not a great starting place for building a solid foundation for a good strong lasting friendship or relationship. So, the way you go into developing a friendship should be based on truth and not withholding things back.

If you started or wanted to get close to me the door and the opportunities would shut down quickly. If you disappointed the Ambassador, you would take a nice long trip something like a hideous not to ever return. If you could not understand my needs, wants, and concerns I called you selfish and I would shut down on you purposely. That's just the way it was while I was acquiring new spirits and souls. I was loving the company but still being emotionally dead to certain feelings not truly allowing the situation to grow into anything beautiful. Being left emotionless not fully giving myself to a person. I was living through my abandonment issues which were based on me pushing people away if they didn't play by my rules or fit into my box along with certain comments, actions, thoughts, lack of focus and their mindset.

Many days and nights I found myself counseling others giving them love from different perspectives, showing different ways of thinking and how to properly perform a certain task. The people I was helping loved the outcome as a result of the coaching and counseling which boosted their self-esteem and confidence that was low when I met them. I know I have the gift of which allows me to read people and to know things that are not spoken so I thought. I was good at seeing situations before they happened and knowing when to push and love on people in their personal life or professional life. Plus, when you grow up in a strong environment, your thoughts are your own and there is no room for weakness that would be used against you. The strong survive, you suck up your feelings and emotions, grind and sort your feelings out later when you are alone. If I be honest, your feelings never get sorted out, they just become a part of who you are along with the teachings you may receive from family, friends, church folks and the streets.

Mental and emotional toughness is taught and a form of learned behavior you must always display it. Now don't get me wrong, love and emotions are important but there is a time and place for everything. If you were to show signs of weakness or being in need, it could lead to you being attacked or destroyed. Now this is a mindset that I displayed once in my life because people are taught and witness certain things which become an important aspect of their mind growing and developing. Regardless if it was based on your own doings or not, your thoughts guided and covered who you were.

Everyone has had some thoughts and thinking patterns that have changed the course of their life. The fact of the matter, it is about changing where your mindset was then and even now, it should always be about improving and expanding yourself to newer and greater levels of listening, accepting, healing, focusing, loving, enduring, releasing, enjoying, happiness, accountability and tapping into your power. The goal is for people to no longer see you, but see the greater power moving through you. As the greater power consumes your life, you will completely change, it will be lifestyle and your purpose in life.

Pieces of the Promise

- Understanding the Promise
- Listen before you speak
- Choose the right words
- Live the Promise
- Add welcoming words to your vocabulary
- Define the Promise
- Ask open ended questions
- The Promise has been giving to you since birth
- Demonstrate empathy along with morals and values
- Make eye contact
- Put your best ear forward
- Learn to customize your connections with each person
- Maintain positive inviting posture
- Appreciate others and learned to be appreciated
- Eliminate distractions and foolishness
- Make sure your tone matches the message you are attempting to deliver
- Respect the struggle and the path it's all a journey of development to the Promise
- Your individual promise does not live in others it belongs to you
- God has placed your promise in your soul cultivate it and release it
- Deliver the Promise

Poetic Reflections

<u>I Promise</u>

I promise to be strong so that nothing can disturb my peace of mind

My Promise is to make as many people as I can feel that there is

something special in them

To look at the positive side of everything and make my optimism

come true

To be just as enthusiastic about the success of others as

I'm about my own

To learn from the mistakes of the past and press on to the greater call-

ing, achievement of the future

To have a cheerful presence always and give every living creature I

meet a smile and be courteous to them

I promise to put so much time and effort into the improvement of my-

self that I dare not make or have time to criticize others

I Promise

To be grateful not to worry, to noble for anger, too strong to fear, to be happy to permit the presence of trouble to enter my spirit and

consume me

To be a light for others not judge

To stand when others will not

To have the faith and keep holding on regardless of the situation

To have life is a blessing and now endure the obstacles and

enjoy the journey

I promise to uphold a standard that cannot be shaken

The path that I'm on is the promise God has for me

My purpose is to sow greatness and beauty into life of others who

don't believe

Failure is not an option

I have no choice but to step into my purpose and greatness

And help you discover yours with love and truth

Chapter 2

The Struggle Within

Many of us search for ultimate love and peace through life's journey, whether it's a career, for a husband or wife, kids that are healthy and doing good, finances, love, passion, happiness, great sex or just a piece of mind. The thought plays in my mind like a soliloquy of drama mixed with music. Many have attempted to master their struggle within, so they say or think as their thoughts circle around in their spiritual being. Honestly, it's a challenge many struggle with daily. Doing their best not to go backwards to the places in their life which had meaning. The places which lead to them learning and experiencing pain and hurt such as the streets, cheating, drugs, alcohol, fighting, cussing, self-sabotaging themselves or family and the list goes on and on forever. Any type of damaging, troublesome, disrupting behavior will sum up the pain and hurt.

Truth is everybody is dealing with something and has acquired certain tools to help assist them along their journey better than others. Then you have a group of people who are attempting to manage their struggle within in a different form. Many people have not overcome certain struggles in their life and the internal struggle is often the hardest one to either grasp or get a handle. It is especially hard if you're in denial and don't have a clue how to approach the struggle within. There are individuals who are fighting every day and still are struggling with their individual internal monster. The struggle within can be so many different things you do to yourself and allow to penetrate your spirit and body or things you are not aware of.

Take this leap with me in this chamber of thinking but just a helpful note sometimes the struggle within can be assisted with a new way of teaching, listening, loving, help, assistance, focus, and praying. The goal in life should be to love yourself better and to love others better in life. Healing is one of the keys along with doing some serious soul searching and battling with yourself and thoughts. It is very important to equip yourself with other tools and weaponry to help yourself and others. Self-preservation is good, but equipping others around you can display something many people, communities, families and a life-style of essentially freedom, growth, and joy this world is not accustomed to.

Often people go through a giving up period in their life, relationships, marriages or anything they have any attachment to. The breakdown of communication, trust, honor, respect, the wiliness to fulfill each other needs, concerns and happiness also plays a part. The struggle within theory deals with giving things up. In life we will all have to release our hand just like playing cards. Life deals you several different hands you must play out, but the importance of the hand is how you maneuver through the process of what's in your hand called life. The struggle aspect is what we pick up as individuals and learn in life makes and defines us. Some of us grow and mature while some just grow old but never grow up mentality, spiritual and financially.

My colleague, Romero Spates, once told me Vick we have a brought lesson. I sat for a moment processed what he said to me. He elaborated and shared some of his brought lessons with me. Romero broke it down to me with several different meanings; he flat out told me Vick I had to learn, and I paid for each one of my lessons dearly with my life. When you think about that's the struggle within us. We buy certain lessons then when it's time to pay up as humans, we don't fork up the penalty. We want it on credit or layaway and the master teacher does not allow us off the hook. The struggle is often God has given us warning signs we ignored. The warning signs were supposed to speak to us or he places people in our life to show and teach us which we often ignore or just turn a blind eye.

So, what is it? Well, you must be honest with yourself and ask the question. I never understood that part of the relationship and the point when people say the most misused universal word of all times... I love you, they love each other or I'm here for you. It all breaks down to whatever phrase, attitude, statement, conversation or the I don't care attitude. In relationships, people honestly believe in their creative minds and internal worlds that he or she is not going anywhere, I'm not worried if they leave. If that isn't being arrogant, confident, stupid, or just downright comfortable in your current situation, I don't know what it is.

We have not scratched the surface to the struggle within which aligns with the brought lesson and how we as human beings need to release our hands. Your mindset and dead seeds planted in your mind and heart are the foundation of it all. Whatever has been planted in your mind and heart has not produced anything lush, productive or fertile. You are stuck in the struggling phase of your life and relationship. Or maybe you have all the answers because you are listening and opening yourself up to new ways of thinking. You may be more mindful of information or not ever becoming too comfortable that you take people and life for granted. Maybe this is not your thing. Many of us are just not willing to change something in ourselves, but you expect a different result. I guess since it has been working for their grandparents, kissing cousin and a long line of generation curses it's no need to do anything different. So, you think?

Your struggle may be different but it's something you have been toiling and fighting with that has stopped your growth and determination. You must attempt to fix things because maybe that is the role and position God has placed in you to handle. Regardless if it's pain from the past, bad family relationships that never grew as you wanted them to or trauma you have endured over the years, it is preventing you from loving yourself and others effectively. You have done well at masking the problem, but you are self-sabotaging yourself and secretly hating and despising the growth of others. You can't stand to see people happy that are doing things differently than you. You have become a sideline complainer.

Release your hand from any more foolishness, painful thoughts or attitudes about it; you did your part to fix the situation and yourself. Stubbornness, selfishness and being stuck is not of God, that is all part of being human and closed minded. Not being flexible and the unwillingness to bend for yourself and others can place you in your own internal struggle within which may lead to a landfill of trash and space. What's in a landfill? Just a bunch of stuff people do not want. It stinks, full of rubbish, and all types of creatures. Birds see it as a sovereign territory to see what type of scraps they can find. The bottom line is it is a dumping ground for disposal of waste, a final burial.

Often the bread pieces are all that is left in this circle of life which is your heart. Once or twice in this life, some of us have reached rock bottom. Rock bottom is the process of losing everything that might have been important to you. It might be your life being torn down or the place where you completely lost your way. You just don't know how to get out of your own way. I personally had to fall in love with rock bottom. I love my rock bottom because I could see who would be there for me during this trial and stormy season of my life. Sometimes it is good for you to face it alone. I had no choice but to grow, fight and release certain things and people because if I didn't, I would have been dead. People will laugh, joke, throw subliminal jabs and isolate you. Pretty much they will write you off. Being at rock bottom is a different kind of task and focus which illuminates the struggle within. Rock bottom is probably the hardest fight you will ever face as a human being. Do you know why this is the hardest fight of your life? You must endure you and your choices. It is not a self-pity moment but a movement that you should take in your individual journey of life and rationalization. Making excuses or blaming others will never bring you out of your rock bottom.

The struggle within and rock bottom is an accountability phase. You must detox your life and empty out plenty of waste – unhealthy thoughts, lies and false truths. Your current conditions are echoes of your past choices. What choice and decision you make will help you process why you are stuck, unsatisfied and struggling. You are frustrated for a reason; this is part of the process to unleashing that purpose that has been hidden and detained. You are in control because it is decision-based, you can envision, feel or believe it.

I have worked with different populations of kids and adults through advising, counseling and just being an active listener. When sharing with groups and individuals the only thing that you are in control of is your behavior and how you choose to react and handle the situation. Peeling off the layers, being numb to the lies, renewing your mind and reflecting on your rock bottom experience is attached to how change greatness then you evolve. Never not see the potential in yourself even through the storms. Though the clouds may dampen your sight, do not let it make you put your vision on the shelf. The rock bottom and struggle within are a learning process, releasing stage and reliving certain phases of your life.

You may ask yourself why I did that or why did I allow this to happen, it's called second guessing. Do whatever you have to, to fight, battle, walk and focus through it. There are so many levels to the struggle within, but you will need to do some soul searching and take the time to start recognizing certain behaviors and actions to release them. The struggle can be accepting things you should not, conversating about things which you should not even take the time to entertain or consuming things into your mind and spirit. It's time to dig deep into your inner soul and reflect, but when you start deflecting and pushing those thoughts out. Beware though. As you dig, you will dump on other people and create your own personal blackhole. You will self-sabotage your growth and development.

Every professional began as an amateur. You must start somewhere; take the journey. There is a spiritual part to your inner struggle, but let's be clear, you do not get a pass or make excuses, they are not acceptable. Just because you are struggling does not give you the right or opportunity to be rude, nasty or disrespectful to other people. Laziness, excuses, and denial are like adding fuel to the fire which is the struggle within and a catalyst to rock bottom. One thing we must do as human beings while going through our individual struggle within is to stop making things more difficult for yourself. How so? Remember to release your hand, release those negative people and energy around you. Let's just say let go of the drama. You will need to let go of every and anything that will prohibit or not allow you to grow or have peace, love, and support. Not having those needs and discipline equals death defining distractions and life-altering traumatic events which feed the struggle within.

Poetic Reflections

Release My Hand
As the flowers die

We still say goodbye

No lies were ever uncovered

Time was the issue

Longing for a visual view of you

So, you had to dismiss the other person

Love was in the air

But then people's emotions thoughts filled the atmosphere

God what happen to me?

What happen to us?

No trust a lot of lust

No one would ever just hush to hear the other crying out

of their heart

No one would ever hush to hear from you Lord

People are not playing their roles and part where not achieved so

old thoughts and behavior

Will proceed to enter

As I cleave to something new

I never really had the chance

To Love you through it all

Regardless of the pride or hurt that would not

Allow the hands to turn back the hands of time

As I dream and close my eyes I will remember you

The Story to the struggle within

I wake, and I fight me

More than I fight others

My soul shatters within

I have seen the hate from others

It burns inside

The whisper is strong

It's a struggle

It's a hustle

The pain is even stronger

The hell is even deeper

That you will endure

If you don't decide to change your

Respect yourself

Break free and breakthrough

Be your own visual of love, passion, and dedication

My layers have been exposed

I see the walls closing on me

I fight, or others more than I fight for myself

The way I choose to heal is stealing my joy

The foundation is me

I keep losing the moments

The moments of peace

And aligning myself with my designer and forgiver of all

Chapter 3

Birth of Deception

Whatever your title, position or views are as a professional, parent or a supporting factor in society know we are losing our young princes. A child transitions to a teenager, young adult, and then an adult, but may not reach their full potential. Let me reiterate again, we are losing our boys and men. No matter if you are a good parent or not, don't have kids, are single, married, whatever it may be, as a culture and society we are losing them collectively in masses. Many of our kids have been thrust into positions they are not ready for mentally, physically, or prepared for. The family structure today is just trash and has failed a lot of our kids. Let me say it again, the family structure today has failed our young men. There are not enough men to fill in the gap to teach, support and raise up our young boys. Why? Because men are just not there.

Let's be clear, it's not about buying and spending money on things; it's about spending the one thing in life you can and will never get back...*TIME*. Everything in life is about balance. Please do not get me wrong, my purpose is not to offend anyone or beat you up as a man. I am a man and understand the importance of a man's presence. A man's presence is needed to help, support, and teach our young boys. We are needed to assist them through life when they make mistakes and encourage them in a different light. Men provide different perspectives and insights than a woman. My voice as a man is different from a woman and it is not to say both are not needed or important, but our boys need the family structure to change. It is not fair for our kids to be fighting generational curses that our fathers have laid, and they are not here to assist in the developmental and supporting stages in their life.

Now let's turn our focus to support. Support is universal and both men and women need it. Support is different for each person and valuable. It cannot just be one-sided though; all key factors have to be present. If one factor is missing or not in the picture because of selfish reasons or just choices, then we are paving the way to continue losing our young men. How can we expect them to become successful kings when they have no support? We are living in an era where there is no structure and discipline, just reality TV and social media. Family structure means we sit down and have a meal at the kitchen table without the television on or cell phones. Homes are lacking wisdom. The older generations are no longer around to give sound advice such as grandparents. Today's grandparents are on Facebook, in their 40's and still clubbing trying to dress like the young ones. They are looking and searching for something or someone.

Once upon a time, you could turn on the television and multiple shows provided examples of healthy family dynamics, issues, and structures. Unfortunately, today this is not the case. Changing the conversation, language and structure of home opens the way for trauma, drama, abuse, abandonment, lack of support, substance abuse, no discipline, and no value of education. These things often come from the ones who are supposed to be protecting kids and enriching their lives as adults.

The reason we are losing our young men is a combination of factors. How important is it for a man to just have a conversation with a young man, teach him how to tie a tie, talk to him about how he should keep himself groomed, or how to be respectful at all times especially when he is speaking to a young lady and women. To teach him that he is strong and handsome, but it is okay to have feelings and not to mask them. How to handle and manage his anger when he's upset, to be careful who you associate yourself with and allow into your circle. Teach a young man to have a plan and develop goals with multiple options and not to put all his eggs in one basket. Teach him to be mindful, work hard, and grind for himself and his future family. Teach him to set priorities, not wants or immediate gratifications. If a man does not work, he does not eat. Teach him not to give up or quit on himself. These simple conversations are not occurring and plenty more conversations need to be discussed about life. Unfortunately, it will not happen because so many young men are detained and locked up. All too often the incarcerated system teaches our young men new ways to mask their frustration and not how to make changes to become a man.

Our young men have no sense of identity and no idea of what a man looks like or should represent. The only examples they see are rappers, athletes, or entertainers. This lack of or no sense of identity has had a historical effect on them who have become old boys-men behind bars. They never grow up or change because no one has helped them in ways that are beneficial. Let me explain even more, it should not take our boys and men to be locked down in the criminal justice system to pick up a book to read for their minds to expand. It should not take a boy or man to be locked down in a cell to take the time to work out and find other ways to sow into their temple that has been made in the imagine of God. Boys and men are visual so why do you think most boys and men are attracted by what they see which will bring attention the expensive clothes, jewelry, cars, and the beautiful women. Men need to be honest with themselves. They desire and crave attention; some want it more than others. For example, the feeling you have when you get a fresh haircut, when you put on a suit, or when a woman tells you that you smell amazing. Those are just a few examples men don't like you to know. If you do not like the word want or like the interpretation of the word attention, then let's use the word acknowledge or recognize by their efforts.

If our men like and enjoy complements what do you think our young men need. So, if my ideology of a man is somebody who has all those things I want and seems important, I do whatever it takes to obtain those same objectives. We place so much value and importance on the wrong things. We place value on symbols and being the center of attention. Whores have cost us so many of our boys and men that they have done many un- humanistic acts. The results of their actions have cost them their freedom and life behind bars. Often times they have the opportunity to return back to the community, but the facts are how often do we throw people away who are different or who have made a choice different from us. Many of us do the number one thing which causes separation; we judge others instead of seeking to understand why. How much does it cost to listen or have a conversation to find ways to help and assist? Many have missed out on life and love, but certain choices and situations have lifelong damaging consequences and outcomes. Young boys and men have been slowed down or stopped in their growing phase. There are things in life they will never experience because of a choice or decision that has taken them away from their families and communities.

By being a counselor and working with young boys and adult men populations, I have had numerous conversations about the lack of men and teachings they received. Words that were spoken and given to them about life were tainted with poisons, generational curses, and destructive behaviors. Conversations leading to bad advice gave poor perceptions of life and others. There is no gray area. Whenever bad teaching exists or someone is not given the proper tools and understanding, the next generation is subject to the same devastating cycle. Your intentions mean nothing; it boils down to either results or excuses.

The lessons and mistakes you have endured has help to shape who you are as a man. As men, our job is to make better attempts to teach our boys and young adults and provide wisdom jewels. Jewels are words of wisdom, encouragement, empowerment, and lessons of strength based on experience and circumstances. The driving purpose to loving each other better is to help as many individuals as you can. It does not matter if they are family or not. A man's triumph comes from doing things with a purpose, not because it is forced, but because something in his spirit has been awaken. The awakening of his spirit, mind, and soul is a result of the scars and pain he has faced in his life. Through experiences, not knowing God, and someone else pulling you to the side having several come to Jesus moments with you, where would you be in your life's journey. Did somebody just choose to love, help and support you by chance? The fact is we all have made mistakes; we all have had our mind and heart dead to certain things.

Many of us did not have those moments when a father, uncle, cousin, stepfather or a male figure came into your life and shared with you. Many of us did not have the elder statesman, the OG. But those who were blessed to have a father figure and listened to them may have been the game changing moment in their life. I know in a young boy's life there are many circumstances that caused them not to hear a male's voice. See mommy, grandmother, and auntie all have done their best to bring you to a certain point in your life, but it's the only voice you've ever heard. What has become difficult for boys who grow into damaged men, is when they have not had any male voice speak to their mind and soul. Certain pieces are needed to shape, teach, and cultivate a boy into a man, and if these pieces are missing, it will be evident when he becomes a man.

Many adults have told me kids do not listen or they are angry when I teach classes or present information. I am not making excuses for kids, but as adults we do not listen either. Someone kept pushing and believing in you as a kid, why can't we do the same for the younger generation. Unfortunately, some youth have taken roads which have been very difficult and dark. It is a state of emergency concerning our young boys. They believe they can drink, use drugs, steal, commit crimes and be uneducated and still have a prosperous successful life. Risky behaviors have become their value system, along with taking chances with their body and freedom. It is their way of thinking, which is all mixed up. Young boys today do not have discipline or knowledge of themselves. The 'I don't care' attitude they develop leads to 'cell mate dummies' and more plots in the cemetery.

One thing I've learned while doing counseling by going to trainings, workshops, and listening to other scholars, is a therapist are just people with extra titles and alphabet letters after their names. Inside of these meeting rooms, people come up with inventive ways and programs to address some of these issues and concerns of our boys. However, until we change the family structure and start having relatable conversations with our young boys and adults change will not happen. Simply become a good listener and give the unconditional love and support they have never felt. Until we take different approaches and strides, we will continue to lose one of our valuable resources which is the development of a strong man. A person can tell when you care and genuinely are concerned for them. Being genuine means you can sow into someone and not expect anything back. You whole heartedly want to see them reach their full potential and purpose.

A lot of times all the different strategies professional people observe, read, and research from statistics, sometimes causes them to miss the mark. We need to be open to various ways of helping, enlightening, encouraging, supporting, growing, teaching, parenting, loving, pushing, and healing. Let me reassure you, I am not disrespecting or minimizing any contributions that have been made to the world of human services, but I am saying take another look. It can be very easy to lose sight of what's going on when you are sitting behind a desk and complaining about things. If you made a choice not to be on the frontline, you are missing the whole picture. Losing touch can cause professionals to miss the mark, regardless of their experience or understanding. If we do not adjust, we will miss the mark of reaching our boys to help cultivate them into great men, leaders, fathers, and husbands to guide the next generation.

So, let's recap what are we feeding our children's mind? It is very important to show our boys and young adults support, love, and being mentored by a man is very important at each developmental stage of his life while he is growing, learning, and making mistakes. A man's voice is essential to a young boy or man to say I love you and I got your back. Telling them to get up on your feet and look at a person in the eye when you are speaking, and listening is important. Also teaching young boys and men its ok to get up but reaching your hand out in compassion is whole another level of helping and loving each other better. Listed below are some things young boys and adults have shared with me in counseling sessions:

1. I need money
2. I want to be respected and accepted by all people
3. High fashion clothing

4. Jordan sneakers

5. Music I want to be a rapper

6. The hood/environment

7. Video games

8. Girls

9. Robbing

10. Pain and Trauma

11. Drugs/Alcohol

12. Unprotected sex

13. Lack of fathers and positive male influences

14. Criminal behavior and activity

15. Peer relationship in the street

16. Glorifying the wrong things

17. Guns

18. Gangs

19. Think losing your freedom is a game and a joke

20. Sees no value in education

21. Hates to pick up or read a book

22. Nobody cares and I don't care

23. Blind loyalty loving and build bonds with the wrong people

24. Tattoos

25. False Identity

The problem is our culture and the entertainment placed on television, radio and other media. We have not glorified present day heroes or leaders from the past but replaced that with glorifying drug dealers, fast money and people who are corrupt that poison the community. We empower the negative hustle which continues to kill our culture and families. But where is the energy and grace to influence the next generation with proper tools and essential food to feed their impressionable minds.

I'm sure it is much more but this is what has been placed in these young boys and men's minds and spirit. What happens when we push education, living healthy and loving our neighbor? What if more people did less preaching and did more hands-on teaching and encouraging? One thing I have learned from growing up and even in the counseling books, sometimes self-disclosure is needed and can be utilized as a formable asset. Self-disclosure is a teaching strategy not to harm brag or boost but to teach, advise, and uplift with purpose and meaning. As angels placed on earth to do God work, it's our job as adults not to give up on people in general. Unfortunately, how can you love someone better when unconditional love is not present. We must replace this selfish situational love people have and display daily which if it's no longer beneficial for them they are gone. This form of love plants the seeds to death nothing great will become of it; fruit can't grow so there is no harvest of greatness.

We are great when we help transition our young boys and adults to fulfilling their potential to be great. Teachable and coachable moments can lead to cultivation. There will be showers which equal pain, but without the showers and pain how do we grow and learn from our mistakes of not being there teaching our next generation leaders. Pain is triumph and victory. Pain sends a message to the body which sends a message to the brain. The body alerts the brain. The brain typically wants to shut down as a defense mechanism because it's uncomfortable and to protect from further pain. This is where you come into agreement as an individual to choose their lifestyle and tell their brain not to shut down. Nothing is wrong with the body; your body is loving its new experience which is called change. As your mind becomes stronger so does the body. These two become comrades working in unison, one body one mind. This is your journey on how to love oneself and others better, to take it by storm and prove to those who say it's impossible that anything is possible you put your mind to.

Poetic Reflections

Men are essential and needed too

We are lost without you

The fight has been here

Which has emerged into a battle of our lives

We need you our Kings to teach our boys to become soldiers for

them to mature and transition into warriors

You have been told you are no longer needed or important

You have been told your presence doesn't matter

Oh, how we need our men

Oh, how we need their presence

Their voice and guidance

Oh, how we need you to step in the gap and bridge it

We need you to stand and express the vision that has been placed

in you by the higher power

Our families need you the missing key and piece of the puzzle

Our communities desire your words of wisdom

Life Lessons

Oh, how we need our men

Oh, how we need our men to embrace others when needed to, no-

tice the wrongdoings, take charge and teach

We need your hand to pull another man up to teach resiliency not

to sit in silence

Chapter 4

Cultivating Minds and Soils

Growing up and being from the south in Fayetteville North Carolina, you tend to learn about cropping, soil treating, planting seeds, growing, nurturing and cultivation. I remember having to get up at 4:00 am in the morning to pull weeds out the yard and gardens and cutting the grass before the sun came up. I learned how to plant and treat the soil, remove weeds and grass, planting seeds, watering the lawn and the garden. How do you treat your soil= soul? What are you feeding the land= your mind? One thing with this process you learn to have patience. Maybe it's one of the reasons why I wanted to become a counselor, why I look at myself as an Ambassador, why I pledge my life of service to help others and sowing seeds into other people. The cultivating process of loving and helping others is patience, but the groundbreaking based mentality and preparation. Nothing just sprouts and springs up overnight, it appears and develops suddenly.

A goal of this journey of how to love other people better is supposed to be a life of selfless service to others mixed with inspiration. If more individuals learn how to cultivate their own personal gardens and lawns, we could start minimalizing so many issues which have plagued our lives, families, health, mental health, love, life, and spiritual relationship. This is what cropping is. Maybe we should turn off all the drama, reality TV, social media posting liking, gossiping, lying, fighting, and understand you only have one life to live. No one knows when their time may come and it should be the utmost priority to live and cultivate your heart and mind. Sow love into others instead of hate and unnecessary foolish. Align your crops up and treasure the one life you have been giving and blessed with. Every day may not be pleasant, but it depends on your perspective and maturity level. There is beauty and blessing in hardship and stress. Think about it, you are still alive and in your right mind. Mentally, we as human beings take so many things for granted; what often happens from time to time the things that we take for granted, we lose and are taken from us. Cultivating the mind and soil is about healing and meditation. I ask you what is wrong with living the best life ever for yourself and being an example for someone else?

Cultivation is about preparing your crops and land, which equates to your mental health. Your crops are your family, the land is the community and the people who live in the land. The harvest is the children who develop into adults and become successful. The fruit of the labor is how they keep striving and thriving. There is nothing new under the sun, but we must take several different approaches to reach the next generation for them to harvest successfully. No matter how they upset, disappoint, and do not listen, we have to install discipline, value, and self- accountability in their minds and hearts. We have to get back to the basics of time and being patient.

Sowing into people and welcoming the good, the bad and indifferent is part of the cultivation period of loving and helping others. Detoxing things from your individual life that does not enrich your spirit and life is also important. For me, cultivation is about change. If

I have been using a certain method to get things to grow but it's burning my potential harvest or stunting its growth because I am using the wrong combination of materials. Therefore, I need to ask myself why I keep doing the same thing and expecting a better and different result. My actions and methods have not delivered or lived up to my expectation associated with the work I put in. The point is, I am attempting to reach people I can't relate to.

The next generation is our harvest and we have to have multiple different conversations, discussion about real life and experiences. The way our grandparents and parents raised us was very valuable and sometimes a good building block for understanding values and developing morals or for many, it could have been a stream straight sewage leading to the sewer. Teaching principles and values are essential for growth. Often the elder statements and season veteran becomes frustrated and aggravated to the core and gives up on the harvest which is the youth and our communities. We can never stop teaching, preaching, raising, loving, helping, mediating, serving. Truly and explicitly it all must be a combination of factors, we sow into the soil (soul), enhance the seed of the land, enrich our potential harvest which will be our young princes and princesses that need to grow to become Kings and Queens over the land.

I am sure we all know many adults who struggle with discipline, responsibility, and accountability, who love to make excuses and blame others for their individual choices and decisions. Granted, some may not have been provided the same playing field as you. Some of us are starters, second string, benchwarmers, walk-ons or the individuals who have been cut trying out and striving to make the team. And what about individuals who just watch outside the gate or glance into the gym and have just given up because of circumstances. Which one are you? I was the individual who had the dream, but I never made the team; I was cut multiple times. I took time to reflect on what I needed to improve in the moments I did not make the team. Hard work beats talent every time.

Were you able to follow my analogy? I was cut from the basketball team plenty of times in junior high school. There were many times someone told me I wasn't any good or I was arrogant or thought I was better than individuals on the team. I learned not to give up, to push myself, and to learn a different type of discipline. I may have fallen short a few times, but I always worked my butt off to be better. People around me were always sowing and telling me not to give up. Most importantly, I developed something called resiliency. My resilience was not just for making the basketball team, it was for my life and education in general. Please do not get it confused, I was disappointed in myself but there were some core principles and values that were planted early in me. Even though I was disappointed and hurt, it did not give me the right to make excuses or give up on myself or quit.

Quitting kills and destroys the process because things are not going your way. You are not just stopping and quitting on yourself, but more importantly, others who are watching you. Why am I saying this? Because I made the JV basketball team in high school, but I regret letting what was going on with others alter my personal goals. Instead of focusing on the process/opportunity I worked and waited for, I quit. I was so focused on how other people were being treated and handled, I did not know how to separate my mind and thoughts from it. My purpose was not to focus on how others were being treated, regardless if it was better for them and unfair for me. I had an opportunity to work and change the situation, but my mind and spirit were not cultivated at this point to be patient to keep working and grinding. I took the easy way out and quit. I was an immature boy who did not know how to be personable with others. My sucker approach of quitting prevented me from talking to my coach and walking away from my team. This decision still permeates my thoughts as a man today; I think about how I walked away from my team, the experience and most importantly a chance to grow and get better. The point I am making is not about basketball, even though I love it an playing the piano, but it is about your mind not being patient. No matter if the journey and process are difficult or favorable to the way you want it right now you never stop and never quit on yourself.

Due to my own experience, it serves as my foundation as to why. My why to why I go so hard for people during counseling and having a conversation about the importance of thinking differently. You very well may be the example someone needs to stop being foolish or sparks a new form of thinking and conversation. What would happen if a farmer gave up on the crops because he had a bad couple of acres? Does he just stop working? Support may not come when you want it or expect it, but there are people praying for and sowing knowledge into you. As individuals, we cannot be super sensitive, shut down, arrogant or become angry when you walk away expecting to receive a blessing. People plant seeds of love and hope in you because they see what you cannot see in yourself. You may be too immature and not capable of seeing how great you could be.

Trust me, I have seen rock bottom, been hard-headed, did not listen, was stubborn, and the consequences were severe. Cultivating the mind, the land and harvesting sometimes require us to relocate and get some better materials, placing better individuals on the playing field to work the land or who has a vision in their spirit and not the hand of destruction. A positive mind can only bring positive results in life. This is not about perfection, but it is about placing effort. It is my responsibility to help others and myself. It is my job to cultivate my own personal land and crops, which is me. You need times of reflection and meditation on things that will enrich you. According to the Bible (King James Version) in Romans 12:2, we are not to be conformed to this world: but be ye transformed by the renewing of your mind, that ye may prove what is that good, and acceptable and perfect, will of God. Personally, I detox my mind and body. Some ways I do this is changing my diet, eating less meat, juicing, working out, stop drinking alcohol, getting a manicure and pedicure, and taking all-inclusive vacations. The idea is to take of yourself and your mind. It needs to be a lifestyle of self-care and not just something you do every few months or years. Consistency is the key to lifestyle changes. As small of an act as it may seem, you will be surprised how important it is to your well-being. It really works and helps to rejuvenate my temple and the cultivation of my mind; I can love and help others better to strive for greatness.

There are many known dangers of stress and what we put into our mouth and body. However, everyday people take risks in caring for themselves and blaming others why life is not good. We have to do a better job of loving ourselves and letting life situations and circumstances dictate how we treat ourselves and others. What do you see when you look in the mirror? Are you happy with the land you cultivated, and the things God gave you to govern over? You may be happy, or you may be disappointed with certain choices and decisions, but why as human beings do we allow toxic materials and people into our life. From food, alcohol, cigarettes, medication, or any substances that are slowly killing us from the inside out to toxic relationships, jobs, and careers. It is very important to value yourself and the things you have been ordained, giving focus and purpose to govern yourself over.

What is cultivating your land, mind, and soul? The reality is there are too many people who undervalue what they are and overvalue what they are not. Stop striving to be something you are not and grow from the inside. This process is very impossible without a solid foundation. Make a choice to invest in yourself today. It's time to stop being in denial and lying to yourself and masking the day to day lie and pain that has stained your growth and love. Take the mask off and become genuine, masterful, deliver the brilliance that you possess and learn to love your authentic self. As people, we do not love enough, pray enough, hug enough, embrace change deep enough. Our focus is not strong and the silliness of not wanting to change and grow is deeply rooted in our soil in our land. Lies and false realities have our focus captive. But when you awaken you will realize everything you need has been placed, given, and inserted in your DNA from the day you were born. Purpose is learning how to tap into those enriched parts of your system and impart it into others.

Poetic Reflections

Bias Temporary Love

There will be individuals that will come to steal your

energy and time

What they offer you will be seasonal nothing of any kind

of substance

You will crave and reach out for them

Openness

I want to be close to your soul

You will open up to their emotional darkness and their mask

A task that will be hard to notice and break without you

becoming broken

Excuses upon more Excuses why they can't release certain

people and the past

Attempting to love them has become more a task

They have picked a side regardless if you are aware of it not

The lack of respect will leave you staring off into space

Displaced emotions

Being attached to their thoughts and ways of actions has

empowered them

Fueled their inner being and will always deflect

The mask of denial and being sensitive

Continues to hurt and sting

You are temporary to them

You served a purpose but without no true meaning to them

They will never solely exclusively choose you

But they admire what you represent

Chapter 5

Red Flags

What are red flags? Anything that will alert your attention immediately such as words, language, behaviors, erratic actions, or certain things not right with the other person. The red flag phase should not sit well with you if you are learning how to love each other better. The issue is not that you are better than anybody else, but I'm better for me and it not my job to fix your situation. Stop treating people like they are your personal project, community service or missionary work.

What often happens is you think can fix people. The red flag phase has people thinking in their mind, if they give a person a chance because they are attractive, have a nice body or whatever your thought is of why you entertain this type of foolishness. Listen up, red flags are swigging hard as the wind is blowing on a March day. You will put your morals, values, principles, thoughts, and experiences on the back-burner for outright disrespect and foolish pride.

Several people have the mindset they can change the other person. They have it all planned out thinking they will be ok. But why? Why? Why set yourself up for failure and unwanted pain. We ignore the red flags because he is handsome with big arms or because she has a fat butt with a slim waist. Realistically, the flesh allows us not to pay attention to subtle processing signs or lack of judgment. Here are couple of examples of red flags: he or she still talks and sends text messages to their ex, married but has been separated for months, friendships which do not have or respect any type of boundaries, no legal income coming in, does not believe in saving/investing, gossips about everybody, complains a lot, negative talk, never happy for others, devalues the opposite sex, disrespectful to people, has no problem playing Russian roulette with their freedom just to name a few.

Red flags are any type of behavior a person can use to manipulate or harm you for no apparent reason, but it's of value to the user. This is when you should become an active listener and really take the time to listen and not hear. What is not being said? There is a significant difference when you hear somebody or when you listen to somebody. People have told you some very powerful things, but you may not have fully comprehend or digested the information that was given to you. The information just went over your head.

Red flags are not always presented as disrespectful, but it is covered up and masked with words of grace. Red flags are excuses, not being accountable for your own personal actions, attachments to individuals and their past. It is very important to notice red flags in the beginning because it gives you the opportunity to decide if you want to deal or entertain this person on any type of level. At that moment you will realize if you want to continue or develop further. We are supposed to live our lives in moments. Embracing and growing in each moment at a time will equate to building a lifetime of memories and joy. Also, while you are growing, developing and learning how to love each other better you are displaying and utilizing wisdom. What is wisdom? Well for me it's having experience, knowledge and good judgment which will help develop strong principles, better decision making, judgment and one of the most important things you can use for yourself is common sense.

Now don't get me wrong I do understand nobody is perfect and people do have different ways to communicate their feelings and thoughts. I also understand certain people display this thing called potential where they may be in struggling or laying a foundation to a road of greatness. Please do not get the struggle to be great mixed up with the red flags and excuses individuals use to play games and manipulate you. As you are developing and growing it should not be one-sided or lopsided in which it only benefits one party. Struggling and growing is a process.

Many people are looking for the finished product; everybody loves the sparkling diamond or the beautiful butterfly after the process. Those are the finished products, what about the process and the steps it took these examples to get there. Granted the struggle within does take time, work, and sacrifice. Red Flags are helpful but are very crucial in life development and journey. Would you outright purchase your first home on a weak foundation with structural damages and issues with pest control – mice, bugs, and cockroaches? You probably could because provisions could be made to fix the problems, but you can visually see issues with this potential property. In your mind you say I know there are some things I need to fix immediately. However, this approach works for some people, but not everyone. Knowing you must put work in upfront may be a turnoff. It may be exciting because you are a hands-on type of person. Personally, I am not looking to do this in the beginning stages of major purchases or a relationship. I would rather see and experience certain things right away. It gives me the option to make an impromptu decision on if this is the type of investment or influence, I want to give of myself to this situation. Once again there is no judgment wherever you find happiness, motivation, inspiration, and love then to make it your own. The key is just being mindful no risk no reward. Understand if you sit down at the table to gamble you must also be prepared to lose. Listed below are additional red flag examples.

Red Flag Examples

1. Liars
2. Makes excuses
3. Not accountable for actions and behaviors
4. Denial
5. Rationalizes every situation
6. I know everything
7. Can never be wrong
8. Will not apologize.
9. Has no problem with offending or hurting other people
10. Participated in abusive relationships
11. He or she does not take care of their kids
12. Immaturity
13. Has a sense of entitlement
14. Doesn't believe in God or love
15. Uses several different substances as a coping mechanism
16. Addicted

17. Selfish

18. Shuts down and will not listen to you

19. Walks away from you

20. Inappropriate text messages from the opposite sex

21. Attentive to whores and savages

22. Hypocrite

23. Poor hygiene

24. Cannot keep a house clean or in order

25. No discipline with finances

26. Lack of personal goals for themselves

27. Very judgmental of others

28. Secretive

29. Do what I say mentality, but not as I do

30. Pulls energy from multiple different people

Everyone makes mistakes, I repeat make mistakes. It is not about being critical of people, but it is your responsibility to handle situations, so it does not affect you or someone else. As you deal with red flags know if you allow those things to re-surface it can and will cause drama down the road. The other person also needs to be mindful to have your best interest in mind and protect you. If you make the choice to entertain them and their conflicting spirits and soul ties, know what you are getting yourself into upfront. People who connected and battling within themselves and going back and forth are suspect and dangerous. Prepare yourself now for some immediate disappointments and pain.

The writing is on the wall and all over your face. The pain will become a part of you and letting go will be paramount. As you allow an individual to deal with themselves and their situations in a respectful and timely manner, just know you are fueling the red flag that will eventually smother you. You will not reach a solace, holistic, nirvana sense of happiness and peace.

Slowly and realistically you are headed for self-destruction like mentioned before you feel like it's no big deal until your soul becomes connected and conforms to another soul. Human beings tend to force the issue as well as force themselves on other people, relationships, and love. Timing is everything and so is having a peace of mind. Red flags can lead you down a road to several blessings or keep you hostage in a dark alley. Someone please tell me, why we dismiss that gut feeling based on conversations and people's actions; it is a warning sign. The Holy Spirit is trying to tell you something and we just ignore it, time and time again. I am adamant about this theory because I have firsthand experience with it; I learned these life lessons the hard way.

All my lessons and teachings went out the door when I experienced my personal red flags. My mother always told me to just be quiet and listen, you do not always have and need to say anything just listen and look into a person's eyes. Their eyes will give you the answers and what you are looking for and need. Do not get me wrong this lesson on how to love each other better is very critical. The gift of discernment is a spiritual gift which will assist you in so many ways during your road to greatness and how to love each other better. It will let you know a person is lying for no reason, secretly hating, wanting to set you up or harm you. This is troubling when you are only wanting to show and expose individuals to something they are not used to.

You do not have the have the power to finesse and conform them into your world, because you are the one being transformed and led down a road of heartache and pain. The power struggles and pain come from your own thoughts and that device you keep in your hand. You have the power realistically, but you choose not to do anything with it. The power part you have as an individual is you can decide to ignore it and do nothing with it but develop multiple level of feelings that do nothing for you. There is no growth behind those feelings. The power part is you don't have to entertain it. I repeat you DON'T have to entertain nothing. DON'T answer the phone. DON'T open your door. DON'T open or answer the email. You have the power to demand change and not accept the sucker bull crap that people will offer and give you.

Once again, I repeat when you decide to sit down and entertain the conversation, text messages, or face to face contact you have given up your power. You will make excuses for others and convince yourself because you are kind and have a big heart it makes you border line lame. When it comes to the addiction of the heart and mind don't accept the call, don't make that purchase. There is power in using the word NO and allowing others to receive and process it. It is one of the most powerful things you can do for yourself.

Value is another informative aspect of loving each other better. We all have some level of value placed on things, people we love or appreciate or want to be a part of. Value has always been the bridge that has carried us to the word love or potential like. Throughout history and wars people have fought and died for safety, family, respect, power, religion, love, territory and freedom. In different times throughout history, it is interesting to see what certain people desired and needed along with how they valued those things. The different values each person may have was a result of how they were raised.

As you begin to understand people, you will see their upbringing was totally different at times or comparable to yours. I like to use the thought about people having and using cell phones. The first thing most people do in the morning before they pray or wash the crust out of their eyes, is swipe to check their cell phone. Then they check it again before driving off in the morning. There are some households who have replaced morning sex and intimacy with checking emails and text messages from the night before or the ones you get first thing in the morning. Often the people who are in your phone or who you choose to talk to, or text has some type of meaning or value to you. Think of the people who get most of your time. These people have some prime real estate in your life. Real estate in your life you ask? These are people who have obtained space, time and value to you. You value their time, effort, words they speak to you, and conversation. You have given them some form of importance and residence in your life.

Poetic Reflections

Okay

It's okay to be regular and confident but fabulous as well.

It's okay to teach people how to treat you and how you need to

place them in your life.

It's okay to do things that will better you.

It's okay not to allow people to hurt you.

It's okay to become unbothered.

It's okay to close the door on the past.

It's okay to tap into the excellence that's inside of you.

It's okay to become great and phenomenal.

It's okay to use the word NO.

It's okay to break out of that comfort zone.

It's okay to disappear and enjoy yourself.

It's okay to smile and laugh.

It's okay to find multiple different ways to heal.

It's okay not to allow life and others to steal your joy.

Chapter 6

Sideline Complainers

People are critical, some more than others. Say you are teaching a class, I guarantee someone is watching, admiring, and hating on you. Unfortunately, people will always have your name in everything accept a prayer or anything positive. There are not too many people in this world who truly want to see you happy, learning and growing in several different directions. People will show you who they are. Thank them and God for the opportunity to have experience who they are. We have many people in the world who are just sideline complainers.

The fact is people love to complain, but they will not do anything different. I have spoken about in other chapters how these individuals will not take the necessary steps to change their current or future circumstances. They just want to talk, vent and complain to other people and place their negative opinions on others that will listen.

Sideline complainers will never support you or your growth. The sideline complainer will not seize any opportunities to advance themselves either. They only see it as more work or growing which takes them away from their comfortable in a box lifestyle. Being pulled out of your comfortable lifestyle and your way of thinking causes you to review things differently. It will take growth, time and changing to pull you out of your own way. Sideline complainers will always notice and see the negativity in other people. They make comments like who do they think they are; they sure didn't work for that; I know more than they do; how did he or she get that new position; you don't need all that education; or how did they purchase that. Sideline complainers have plenty of time they will not utilize positively or constructively. Idol time is the devil's playground. Sitting still will allow your thoughts to overwhelm your mind with negativity. Negative thoughts will take you all over the place where you will never focus on the individual which is you.

This is purposed based theory. The issue and concern are internally which allows people to become stuck and stubborn. As a result, people start hating and sideline complaining on your journey in life to love yourself better and others. If you ever watched or played sports on a team you see individuals on the sideline supporting the team. You think they have a common goal to win the game and hopefully to win and obtain a championship. Everybody on the team and on the sideline are working together from practice players, benchwarmers, current players on the roster, those playing and the coaches. But now remember this is not little league where everybody gets to play because their parent paid for a jersey and trophy. There are individuals waiting for someone to get hurt so they can step in and take your spot. There is a big difference when you step in and step up when somebody gets hurt. Make sure you take advantage of the opportunity because you have been preparing yourself and you are ready to rock. But the flip side is when you are patiently waiting on someone's demise. This type of sideline complaining and thinking happens in all areas of life such as relationships, employment, sports, careers etc.

Generally speaking, sideline complainers do not understand your way of thinking; they will either befriend or fear you. Do understand they will do whatever they can directly or indirectly to attempt to destroy your character. Truth is sideline complainers are preparing and coming to do all of what I just mentioned to purposely end you or to witness your break down. This gives people like this a burst of energy to their ego and gives them something else to talk about. Sideline complainers often will not say anything to you directly, they will talk and make comments around you or to other people. You must also remember everybody is not built like you or have the same level of morals and principles.

A sideline complainer will watch the enemy prepare, discuss and attack you and never mention anything to you until after the fact. Pretty much they wait until the damage has been done and may possibly make comments such as I thought you knew I heard that long time ago. They will not share anything with you no information, just another conversation piece for them. Sometimes sideline complainers are always talking about others during any circumstance or situation. Please listen to what are the sideline complainer discussing. You will probably never hear them say how they can improve on themselves.

You can deal with sideline complainers by not seeking anyone's approval because you develop you own power within. Remember you do not lose people, you lose people who never liked you, never respected you, never cared about you, never loved you. That's why it is so easy for people to hurt you, leave you, disappoint you, attempt to damage and sideline complain about you. The fundamental and foundational perspective of care, support and love was never there. If it was, it was tainted with some other hidden aspect that you were not aware of.

Learn to respect the hidden jabs and the direct and indirect comments. Those are your red flags and warning shots about certain things placing you on notice. Learn to evict those sideline complainers from your life. Once again for those who watch and know sports jargon, think about once everything is said and done remember the people who were on the field and in the locker room after you lose. You might not notice and recognize certain things when you are winning and on top. Stop thinking other people are supposed to be your motivation, especially not a sideline complainer. They cannot be your motivation until you get yourself together and right.

On this journey of loving yourself and others better, focus and purposefully align your attention to distractions and people who wish to take you off your game. Hatred is real. The sneaky dissing will continue to happen directly and indirectly. As you grow and change, the plotting to take and discredit your hard work and efforts and to create and make changes will not cease. You must make the decision how it affects you. People will inspire you or they will drain you. Pick people in your life wisely. Sideline complainers are in their position by choice and they are supposed to offer what they offer absolutely nothing. Take nothing personally and remember they were never put in place to support or help you.

Sideline complainers are just there to watch and complain about everything you create and develop. In this process of loving each other better, do not use anger because you will have allowed others sideline complaining and hatred control your thinking and the moves you are planning to make. Just listen to their words and watch people's facial expressions. Learn to stare into their eyes and soul and always observe their body language. Be mindful of the words you are putting out there. Hear what is being said and not being said, therefore you can interpret the silence and energy that is being placed in the air. Remember you are loving others better, but you are loving yourself as well. Do not hold grudges, just remember the facts.

You are in a transitional period in your life. Focus on loving others better. This is your growing period. Time to grow, mature, and recognize in your new season of life people and unproductive situations no longer fit into your space. They have no place in your life and must fall away. Stop fighting the process of releasing people or watching the sideline complainers not support or have love for you. You must become unbothered as you take this journey of learning to love others better. To get to a place of being unbothered, you must cut off unnecessary people, places and things.

As I speak with juveniles, we have these types of conversations where I express to them there will be people in your life who will try and test your patience daily. People, family, friends, complete strangers and the world we live in will probably not have faith or support you. What you are striving for cannot be hindered by attitude, interactions or the mistakes you have made in the past. God places sideline complainers in your life to push and make you stronger. Just as he puts the right people in your life to assist and give you directions as well. Trying to balance our lives as individuals we tend to or have difficulty seeing and feeling helpful harmful situations. Consequently, they were all tools of growth to test your goals and visions through the lack of support and sideline complaining.

I recall the moment when I told some family and friends I was going to work on my master's degree in counseling. To be honest, I struggled in school because did not pay attention. I was more focused on being the class clown and being a comedian. Ironically, when I worked on my master's degree though, I was working three jobs in the mental health field and drove every other weekend from Fayetteville, NC to Myrtle Beach, SC for class. To some people it might not seem like nothing, but to me and my good brother Dr. Albert McMillian, we would not get off from work until midnight or sometimes after then. By the time I would get home and attempt to get situated or try to shut my eyes it was time to get up. By 5:00am to hit the road traveling to South Carolina to be in class by 8:00am to 5:00pm. The blessing is that we supported each other and took turns driving but my brother started the process before me working on his master's degree. The reason I am sharing this is because many people told me we will see how long you will last or not complete the program. The point I am making is there will always be plenty of sideline complainers or people who say you cannot do or make something happen. People I loved and respected were trying to discourage me, but it did not hinder me one step of the way.

During the process of sideline complainers, I had someone going through the process with me until he graduated before I did. So, we supported and motivated each other to keep pushing and grinding no matter what happen. It took discipline regardless if we lived out of town and out of state; we still had to be on time, present and ready to get the work done. You had to be or become a professional with no excuses; it was not allowed. You also could not make any letter grade lower than a C average. For someone like myself who struggled in school, used to eat lunch early with special education classes or grew up old school seeing the students in the white buildings, it was a challenge. I used to go to the huts behind the school because I was labeled and considered special.

This is just one aspect of my journey. I am sure you have your own story and challenges you had to overcome and fight through. The funny thing is I know it helped you to develop and have passion for your hustle and vision. There are people who have the undying feeling and passion burn in their soul. They will not be denied. Do not allow other people to discredit you or your hard work allow this to fuel your dreams. That's what sideline complainers are here for. Distance yourself from the people who lie, disrespect, put you down or have no problem using you.

Poetic Reflections

The Awakening Point

I have been in a cage mentality

Stuck in a dungeon of being unaware

I have been stuck in the normal lackluster

Which has been taught and programmed for me to

embrace and live by

Going through the motion and coasting

Learning the pitfalls and finally listening to the calling of

my soul and spirit

The conflicting converse I had to have with oneself has

been a journey

A journey of torment and anguish

Understanding and feeling the vibe and energy of your life

Why do we find multiple different ways to sabotage

our own life?

Instead of becoming our own personal lifestyle specialist

It's not about the brands

It's about expanding the culture and enriching your life

Having a better quality of life

What you digest

What you tuck close to your vest

This is not top secret its part of the secret principles

Of what you eat and allow into your spirit

Will uplift you or damage you

Chapter 7

Awakening Evolution

Things begin to change when you decide to wake up or have an awakening period in your life. Your feelings and thoughts start to formulate differently. Not to minimize our beautiful women who seem to have awakened periods before men all the time; they have things and situations already prioritized in their life. My goal is to develop young boys into men who can learn to understand and discover some of these principles. Most have not been exposed to them, so I want them to become great fathers and blissful husbands.

A man who becomes awaken is very dangerous. Men who become awoke to have a different type of self-conscience. You think about your community, how you can help others, and consider the things you put into your body that will cause immediate damage or long-term damage. When a man awakes, his focus is not so much on toys, labels, and brands because they care nothing about you. Your thoughts are on financial literacy and educating yourself to change and expand. An awakening opens the door for you to travel to see other cultures and experience different foods, instead of watching reality television. You begin to create your own destiny.

I want to address men who I have previously stated we need so much in this journey. Gentlemen there are many ways you can increase your sexual stock market and your value. This is also about becoming awake. Getting your mind and body in shape, dressing presentable, traveling, getting your finances in order and bettering yourself. My brother Leon Dilligard told me that your bank account will never be mad or upset with you any time you make deposits in your account. You can make different and better options when you have money.

Another value to becoming awoke is being knowledgeable in areas that can help others and being willing to share it with them. Remember this journey is based on how to love each other better; I repeat to love each other better by sharing and exposing others to different options and opportunities. Do not keep things to yourself. Ecclesiastes 4:9-12 talks about how two people are better than one because they get more done by working together. If one falls, the other can help him up. But it is bad for a person who is alone to fall because no one is there to help. If two lie down together they will be warm, but a person alone will not be warm. An enemy might defeat one person, but two people together can defend themselves. A rope woven with three strings is hard to break.

We must break this cycle of laziness and sense of entitlement. We also must learn and except the word. Keep the word and allow it to burn inside of you to fuel your dreams and visions. In my personal journey, some of the best moments happened to be surrounded around the word NO. Some of the material things I wanted as a child or teenager often had the word no attached to it. My parents did not give any explanation, but it came a time where I could understand and receive what they had been teaching and sowing into me. One of my many moments in life to be awoken. They were loving me better in a different way at the time I didn't want to appreciate it.

What I learned from those experiences was to work hard for the things I wanted. It gave me a sense of pride about myself and in my development of growing into a man. I remember wanting expensive shoes and the answer was no. Well let me rephrase it, my mother did buy me the Jordan 4 white cement when I was in 7th grade. I loved them, but she also went and bought my brother Chris the Jordan 4 Carolina blue ones; they were dope. The difference between me and my brother Chris was he was skinny and fresh all the time. Shoes were no big deal to him like they were for me. I was the short, fat, stubby kid. The point is my mother paid for those shoes and vowed never to pay those prices again. Back in those days, Jordan shoes were $100.00 which were expensive especially when you are maintaining a home and kids. My mother gave me a taste of the things I wanted which I appreciated, but it came a time to shop for shoes again and she did not buy them again. I share this not to seem unappreciative or for the people who did not have anything, it was a personal lesson that I learned and value till this day. He helped to push me.

I started my first job at Kroger grocery store where I bagged groceries, took groceries out to people's cars and gathered all the shopping carts in the parking lot. Even before I had a job, I used to rake leaves and I hated it. I walked around several neighborhoods to people houses, asking did they want their grass cut and I even collected recyclable cans. Yes, I could have done all those negative things to obtain money because it was all around me and in my face. That was not the path I wanted to take.

It says something about your inner strength when you have to make sacrifices for the things you want, things you strive for and to go out to make it happen. That is what being driven looks like. I appreciate the word no or the door being closed in my face when I took a chance at sales and network marketing. I appreciate being fired from a job who could not see the potential I had in the moments when I made a mistake. Hearing the word no when ladies did not find me attractive or did not have an interest in me. I appreciate the word no. It took those no's to motivate me to keep working on myself and confidence. I will trust God when I am afraid. God's word is what I will praise and trust. I will not be afraid of what mortal man can do to me according to Psalm 56:3-4.

Keep working to improve yourself. There will come a time when you get tired of asking people for a ride to work or to help you. You will have the means to get your own car. People may be using Uber and Lyft, but there is nothing like having your own. It is nothing like having your own space to kick and put your feet up to relax. I know people loved the roommate experience in college or even renting and living together as adults, but there will come a moment where you will just love and value your own space. There is a serenity when you have your own space you worked, saved up for and made a purchase to obtain. Think about it, people who purchase their first house take a picture with a key standing in front of the sold sign. It is a major milestone for some people that they have accomplished one of their many goals of purchasing a home. This is also part of becoming awake.

Some people make a choice to stop renting to benefit others. They start investing in themselves and their business.

Holistic living, we start once again becoming more mindful of what we put into our system and the medicine that we take. In this system of life and striving to learn to love each other better, some people are starting to become health conscience and focus on a healthy lifestyle. Another part of awakening is not wanting to confine yourself to a hospital bed and taking a bunch of pills daily. Some individuals are making a conscious decision to make a change to being around for themselves and their families. The medicine is in the food we eat and what we read. We mentally should invest in our family and community.

A visual diet is knowing every blessing will cost you something. You will endure and at the end of the trial, it will give you a powerful testimony. Life lessons hurt and come with pain and disappointment, but it is all about overcoming and being triumphant. Everybody's focus is on victory. Becoming awaken has so many levels and dimensions your heart and mind needs to go through. As you discover each level, you will come out changed. You will be closer to God and a holistic person to do his work. This perspective teaches you how to love other people better and still have a love for those who have hurt and crossed you.

I personally recall someone I held to a high standard, respected, loved, and meant a lot to me became toxic over time. They gave me the gift of darkness. It took me some time to understand the gift was a blessing. During my experience with them, I could not understand or see it, but the feelings and emotions were attached to the gift of darkness. I read this the other day and it is such a true statement; you have never been in love until you've begged God to help you let go. This process of loving each other better is a journey but one thing you must realize is it's not always selfishness sometimes it just calls for self-love.

The box of darkness I opened, embraced and fell in love with took me some time to release the pain. The pain tattooed different parts of my soul and thinking. I ate and digested the crap I was given in this period. Like myself, people internalize things that changes your perspectives. You become more mindful of things. Be mindful, certain things can make you bitter, hateful, or vindictive. As human beings, we tend to build our own personal brick walls to protect ourselves and use different defense mechanisms to push people out. The bitterness and pain keep so many people closed and isolated from allowing certain feelings and emotions back in.

A visual diet also makes you think about what you allow into your spirit through entertainment which ranges from what you watch on television, read and things you listen to. Many people will say they have this perspective covered and certain things do not bother them but over time it will. People tend to watch the news every day and listen to a person tell you about a group of people, certain environments, how you live and what to do with your money, etc., etc. Allowing negativity to be pushed into your brain, mind, and spirit tends to fester in your soul and the negativity will eventually come out. Most of the time, it comes out in your relationships, family, and friends during just simple conversation. Daily what you watch on television will and can play a factor in your life.

A visual diet is about balance on your journey of improving yourself and love. It's also about the balance of what you decide to intake into your spirit and mind. If you do not believe it, think about the addiction realm of thinking. You need cigarettes to function, you need a glass of wine to calm down, or you pop a pill to help you relax. If a person watches porn all day every day, they tend to bring those perspectives and practices into their relationship and life. It may cause problems for you because now you have brought your entertainment and fantasy into your reality. And people in your life did not sign up for that.

Poetic Reflections

Awakening Purpose

Get your mind right to be present and open

Heal and develop

Your own mental motivation

Focus on your loved ones before you check your cell phone

and emails

You can plan other people days for work but not take the time

love and take care of your family

Stop giving minimal energy and love to people who are close

to you

Don't make an enemy out of every conversation

Secure your financial freedom

Get your diet and health together

Get your credit together

Drink plenty of water and flush out those fatal toxic poisons in

your system

If you haven't' develop a better prayer life

Money is not everything, but it gives you options

Renew your mind on a daily basis

Allow your mind, body, and soul to release things out of

your system

Write down your goals and look at them and when you accom-

plish one of them mark it off your list and add a new goal to the list

Detox your life

Clear out fake friends and individuals posing as they love you

Chapter 8

Becoming Selfless

Becoming selfless requires one of the greatness principles in life which is called sacrifice. Which is very difficult for many individuals to do for themselves but especially for others. Typically, on this road of loving each other better you will encounter several different emotions and feelings when you are healing and striving to grow. Often the people who are close to you that you love and have respect for might not grow when you grow or have the same vision as you have. This journey and thing called life is so precious and valuable. We do tend to take it for granted and not utilize every moment in life to make ourselves and others that are around us better.

I have realized you should never feel sorry or disappointed for outgrowing people that had the chance to grow with you. This may sound harsh, but it is true when you have shared and exposed others to opportunities and they decline the information. They chose to stop growing and learning, how is that your fault and responsibility. Your responsibility as a leader to support and become selfless as you sow into other people why displaying certain levels and standards. I personally have been around my friends who have exposed me to certain opportunities while on their individual journeys of network marketing and sales. It was not my thing, so I thought, but it gave me an opportunity to grow in so many other ways spiritually and personally that I lacked at that time in my life. There were things inside of me lying dormant because I was too comfortable to unleash them. I decided to fall back from what they were doing because it was not for me. That did not detour them, my friends kept going because it was working for them. The point I'm making is you got to become selfless. Selflessness starts with a sacrifice and there are many individuals out there in the world who find it difficult doing anything that will make them better. You must learn and know what you sign up for.

There are several aspects of being selfless, but I want to share this thought with you. If you can come and eat off my plate and I also can allow you to and you can fix your own plate based on what I'm offering. I can also show you how to get and do the essential things necessary, so you can purchase the groceries you need and like for your own plate. But if somebody puts you on to something, you owe them nothing but the ultimate respect and gratitude. I will not by any means allow any individual to take from me. When certain principles and some good old fashion core developing has taken place along with life experiences, sometimes will allow you to share or allow you to be self-ish and cover all your things to yourself.

The greatest joy for me is for everybody who is in my circle or has impacted and inspired me to eat together and we all be full. But let me take this a step further, my journey and teaching has allowed me to assist and sow into others and give those same selfless acts, principles, knowledge, and teaching to others no matter the cost. I know many people look at self-preservation as you have to make sure you and yours are good. Or you just do not share or risk your name or reputation for the next person. Life has been rough and enduring but through this journey somebody has shown and displayed selfless acts on your behalf which benefit you.

Why do we argue, fight, and get upset about things we can do to make ourselves better? During the holidays people tend to spend and shop in abundance. At the beginning of every new year, gym memberships increase because people focus on working on their physical being. For the first couple of weeks, people state and share with others about their personal workout goals to being healthy. People commit to paying off their debits and bills and saving money for the family during tax time. All these things sound perfectly honest and genuine but what tends to happen is the direct opposite. Selfless is truly a process and sacrifice of self, but often you need to sow into yourself along with being accountable to oneself.

The consistency portion of this is what kills many lives, relationships, and situations. Why are things that can truly make us a better person difficult to change? Knowing my stress level and health will reward me if I work out all year instead of at the beginning of the year. What if we save some money and invest it instead of purchasing things I don't need? Or what if I stop buying things for people who will eventually not appreciate your hard work and effort of wasting money on them. I have experienced and observed that people love just to talk, but do not change or make the necessary improvements.

You are built different and designed with something powerful inside that nobody can take away from you. The worst thing you can ever possible do is to take away the power you have inside your individual spiritual gifts and never use them. To allow life circumstances to consume you to the point that you throw away your gifts or never find ways to tap into them. It takes an act of courage, effort and focus to separate yourself away from just being average and normal. It is important to allow a different level of energy to consume you in your life. Once you realize change is important and inevitable please don't allow your spiritual gift to sit and do nothing with it.

Life is about maximizing and using things you have been given. Being selfless is sharing those things when you give and can open doors for other people. An important but disappointing factor is you will not make yourself or others around you better or successful. Your lack of effort to use your gift is a true waste of a spiritual gift God has blessed you with to help and teach others. Matthew 7:5 (King James Version) says thou hypocrite, first cast out the beam out of thine own eye; and then shalt thou see clearly to cast out the mote out of thy brother's eye. How can you sit there and watch others suffer and hurt? How can you not use what God has blessed you with to spiritually teach and help others? Do not be a sideline complainer that I talked about in previous chapters. Do something that is beneficial and leads to productivity. Move yourself out of your own way.

Chapter 9

Stolen Inspiration and Bipolar Relationships

Often time we give credit to legends or people that have been great, but we have never met them but somehow their greatness has touched or inspired us in many ways. I personally have been inspired by Langston Hughes poetry which is one of the reasons I wanted to write my own poems. I have also been inspired by the words of Nas Jones and the style of Maya Angelou just to name a few. Personally, I have never had the pleasure of meeting these great people except seeing Nas doing some shows and concerts. My point is we channel other people's energy greatness to inspire our own greatness. They have blazed the trails for many of us and opened doors of opportunity to allow us to plug into. As we admire their accomplishments, it allows us to tap into our own inner beauty and creativity.

We all possess the ability to grow, to love and to hopefully love others better. Think about how certain music makes you feel and how you pull a certain kind of energy from it. Listening to smooth R&B makes me feel totally different, compared to when I am at the gym listening to hip-hop. Certain music may put you in the mood to be romantic, intimate or loving. Music changes the energy when you are cooking and preparing a meal for family and friends, and communication is different. Music playing in the background for some individuals makes lovemaking more engaging and powerful at times.

My brother Chris exposed me to the Isley Brothers song Footsteps in the Dark. The song changed my life and I changed as a person. I was attempting to become silky smooth like my brother Chris which I was far from. It inspired me to become who I was in my own light, even though it was still dim. My brother also exposed me to Run DMC, Public Enemy, and the Boogie Down Production. This is probably why I am a decent counselor today because I did a lot of active listening. At this moment in time, I found my own line where I started discovering more and more things that inspired me. I eventually found and purchased my first tape of the great EPMD. This was just an extension of the greatness my brother exposed me to of his lineage of great music which built on the energy of Run DMC.

Inspiration is a powerful thing I recall vaguely listening to Nas Illmatic album, Raekwon and Ghostface Built for Cuban link album. The wordplay and style made me think I could rap but also helped unleashed a creative side of me. I wanted to write down rhymes, poetry, jokes, potential screenplays, love songs, and gospel songs. I started using the pen and pad to write down my thoughts, emotions, lyrics, and goals. Just like reading opens your mind to many different realms of thinking and feeling, that's how I felt. The inspiration came from numerous things that I was experiencing and noticing as I went into a zone, my place of peace.

If you respect someone's success, do not feel ashamed to imitate their successful behavior. Steve Stoute

My experience has allowed me to face many different obstacles in the life of cheers, celebrations, pain and hurt. Also, along the way I have sowed a lot of bad seeds, thinking it is my job to play god and change people. Experiences have taught me I can help, I can love, I can share, I can give and teach but I can't change a person. I just continue to strive and give to people. My experiences have allowed me to be able to share and be a part of many angels' lives. I have had the blessing of experiencing having some amazing friendships that turned into a brotherhood.

The two most important people in my life at the time where Charles Gerald and Derrick Anderson. They were two great amazing men that have gained their wings in heaven. Both of these gentlemen placed a different form of energy, style, grace, purpose, unconditional love and mutual respect into my soul. Out of love and respect, I borrowed and stole inspiration from these guys to help me develop the way I carry myself and handle business.

Experiences like those allowed me to become a different type of person which exposed me to other experiences and for me to have other friendships that have turned into brothers in my life. I met these three amazing brothers in 7th grade, Ray Harper, Vincent King, Xavier Randall. We are always respectful to each other, but we talk trash no matter how old we are. Just like we are still kids at heart. Through our growing up, spending time, obstacles, building a bond, and maturing has allowed an unbreakable circle to form. Whether we were on the same path or different paths, our individual grinds motivated each other in different career avenues.

This form of thinking and maturity allowed me to meet another good brother Albert McMillian in my freshman year of college at Fayetteville State University during summer school. My brother was dressed like Eddie Murphy from Coming to America; I was like who is this negro? But what I come to realize later is he was awake about our heritage and he was from the same place I was from Fayetteville, NC. Albert was such a man of God and displayed an amazing mindset. He was one of the first men I ever met who was a man of God, down to earth, and he would listen to my foolishness. Albert never judged or criticized me. He always made me feel comfortable. We both would share our own personal stories and journeys. What I learned over a period of time that my brother had a high level of pain and could endure so much pain from his own personal life. It never stopped him nor did he ever waiver from his path. I saw and experienced him being a friend and a brother; he always kept it moving in a positive direction even when the chips where down and this was not always in his favor. For me personally, he had my back and understood me.

When I was in the streets whoring, he never judged me, but he always talked and showed me love. I recall having the greatest conversations eating late night dinners after getting off from work as we were working towards our college degrees at Bennigans in Fayetteville, NC. As I was going through my divorce, he was there because he had experienced the hurt and pain I was feeling. He knew what it was like to feel like trash in the court while fighting in a child custody case. The point I'm making is not to put my brother business out there but to share with people the power of a brotherhood. How he and many others shared their words of wisdom and encouragement when they realized I was acting like a lunatic. I was at a breaking point and he had my back. Praying for me and giving me the type of conversations, I needed to break free from the devil's pain that I could not get past.

I love all my brothers. I have utilized and stolen inspiration from people who were in my circle who I had the opportunity to see and spend time with. Regardless if we have different relationships and conversations, each one of my friendships is unique and purposeful. We are all different and made from different fabrics, but someway somehow, we have embraced the differences and it's what keeps us connected. We have the same moral reasoning and compass that was brought us to the things we have embraced and experienced. See we do not talk every day, see each other that much anymore, or always see eye to eye all the time but the power each one of us is inseparable. There is a level of togetherness that exists.

See we saw and spent more time together when we were out in the streets striving to figure this life thing out. From school, the streets, women, relationships, the late-night club runs and mix those with arguments, laughs, and the trash talking sessions. The most important thing each one of us has is individual faith and a belief system that has kept us connected. I almost forgot we have brotherly love and respect for one another. See there is a level of respect I would never ever cross or knowingly hurt or offend my brothers. I will always and forever talk trash to and with them. My loyalty to our brotherhood would never allow me to let an outsider to hurt or address them in a wrong or disrespectful manner.

Their family is my family and vice versa. Vincent King's grandfather, God rest his soul, would always say when he saw me, I never see you until Vince is here. He would always ask me when you are going to get your life together. Well, I'm still working on it, Mr. King. I remember the hours and hours sitting in the back yard talking to Ray Harper's father, Big Ray. I had a connection with him because he was always honest and genuine with me and he embodies all the things my mother would tell and express to me. Big Ray was schooling and catching me up on lifelong lessons that I often would try to fight. The truth is, he was sowing into my soul, but I appreciate it now more than ever.

I have so many stories I can share and express which is my journey, but you have your own experiences. Moral reasoning may have kept you connected or have pushed you to disconnect or dissolve your relationship. The people you start off with often will not complete the race with you. Best friends become strangers instead of brothers and sisters until the end. This journey of loving each other better will teach you and display so many different things to you. Don't allow this to anger or disappoint you, it's just a teaching tool for one of those many coachable moments you will have in life. Just keep living, you will see.

Consistency is the key even though people have different dreams, aspirations, and visions that may not be like yours. Time wasted tends to seep through the door and is a potential gateway to the end. Love is love but family and friends will be the first to hurt and disappoint you, especially when confronted about their behavior or actions. Lack of accountability will allow some people to find different ways to cause trouble and pain which will lead them to disconnect from you. Truth is, they were never with you anyway.

Make peace with God and yourself and stop fighting and struggling with the process. Understand the power you have within you. The wisest person is the one who listens first. I have been saying this for the longest time since I was called into this field of love and helping others that active listening is one of the most important aspects of life and living for others. In this book, we have reviewed this just take some time and listen to people and don't respond. People will display and tell you that they are not on your side and they do not want to be a teammate in business and personal relationships. I have listened to family members, individuals in board rooms talking about business and just listening to women during pillow talk. Some people are not riding for you or will never be you cheerleader which is very important in relationships and growth. I would encourage individuals to take from this perspective not to just watch another person fail when you can assist, encourage and love them through your time, energy and story.

Poetic Reflections

Your eyes say you have given up on me

Your feelings and touch display something different

It seems you have lost your way and love for me

Loving me is not the focus anymore

Your mind is probably telling you to leave me alone

And you will do better and find better for yourself

Then maybe just maybe your heart at times is telling you to

capture what is yours

Something that you are supposed to have with me has been

placed before you

There has been so much struggle and tears

Mixed with our own perception attitude and fears

You don't believe things will ever change nor do you believe

in me

But I don't agree

Love is not enough

But love is the foundation

It's on us to bring the other pieces to the table

But love has kept us together

A kiss has kept us together

The way we would look into each other eyes kept us

The laughing, the hugs, the quiet nights, holding each other

I want you I always have

I have cared for you many years and I have hurt you
so many ways
It seems your heart will not allow you to love me anymore
My quietness I think and know confuses you
I'm silent
Just thinking of ways to make my family love me and try
to make them happy.
And to take care of us clearly, I'm not on the page
of showing you that
All excuses
It's hard for me to hear you can't love now and you are
so unhappy
It's the truth and real
Through it all, I never imagined my life without you
Never saw another woman walking down the aisle to me
Your father giving you away to me
I still love you though I have fought it
I still believe in us
You may not believe in our love anymore maybe it's all a dream
or nightmare now
It seems the pain of having me and the attention and the wanting
of something else
I know I can love you, protect you and support you and
this family

I want to be all you need and for you to be proud of what you
have with me

When hell has entered our lives and relationships so many times

Your smile, your big teeth, your touch, and juicy kisses

Pull me back into proper prospective

Your attitude and sassy ways are hard, but I love certain parts of
that which is you

The makeup of who you are and what you can and will become

Has always drone me closer to your spirit

Then comments and silly actions have pushed us in
opposite directions

You must fight through some bad days to earn the best days of
your life

I pray you open your eyes and heart to me

Chapter 10

Wasted Time

Don't switch the devil for the witch.

Hello Karma, you are being so rude and disrespectful you have

missed a couple of people.

You must be on vacation and relaxing.

Invested time or wasted time…It all depends on what type of individual you are and whom you are dealing with. Some people are an opportunist, some are insecure, some are outright selfish, and some are just downright evil. There are many reasons people waste your time. Think about the times you have invested time and energy into a person, and they end up getting pieces of you and your life. You allow that person into your space, spirit, soul, and thoughts. Then one day, something shifts, and they feel the need to destroy you. I mean they are attacking your spirit being, character, integrity, family, what you believe in; they are out to destroy you. At this stage, they are trying to overwhelm and overthrow who you are and force themselves into your mind.

Some approaches are less aggressive and more sophisticated. Once an individual has taken your mind, they are well on their way to destroying you. Time will make you feel like you have lost yourself in the process. You attempt to hold on to what you had but it is killing you as well. You have to make a decision to hang on and push through to the other side. There is great potential in both of you and you could thrive together. But what did you lose if anything if in the process of accepting potential greatness switched to madness? How important is it to share your thoughts and allow your relationships and friendships into your thoughts and mind? During your journey of learning to love each other better, at what point do you stop allowing yourself to endure the drama, recognize the warning signs, and throw in the towel.

Have you ever wondered why how a pimp can make a woman stand in every type of weather or climate? She walks the streets and gives herself to strangers for sexual services. How can a woman risk her life, health, and safety just to satisfy a person for money? The money she does not keep but gives to a person who abuses her mentally, physically, and emotionally. The reason the pimp can do it is that he has set up shop in her mind. He has planted all types of unfruitful and unproductive seeds in her mind and spirit. For example, the spirit of fear, the spirit of influence, the spirit of intimidation and a spirit of false hope mixed with love and admiration the sparkle on top of all that is knowing how to prey on a person's situation. You have been sucked in just like that.

If we apply this theory to everyday living, life, friendships, relationships, and marriage all too often we repeatedly replay what has happened. We ask the questions what I did wrong or we may blame the other person without really looking at our role as an individual. It is so easy to point a finger at another person but depending on what type of person you are may take the time to self-evaluate yourself and actions. You may even search to discover so innocently your role in the situation.

Now let's revisit the pimp or mind playing games. As stated previously this is the same type of mental games people play in everyday life who may not live in the world of hustling, pimping and sexual favors. Let's take look at the world of people working 9 to 5 or who work 2 – 3 jobs to make ends meet. People use certain things to get what they want, and when they cannot do it anymore or they feel threatened. The abuse monster comes out or the person whose mouth is full of vile and borderline nasty with their words. So, in the everyday world, people use certain comments and tones to get what they want, certain proactive outfits to be noticed, money, and gifts.

Often people have traded sexual favors to move up and advance in their careers. So, apply all these different thoughts and what do you come up with? Maybe you came up with nothing maybe you are confused and disconnected. Why do we as individuals invest our time, money, efforts, hearts into certain situations? Because it is an expectation or a want for something rather. If it is career related to being on a job for years or emotionally wanting to be needed or that feeling of being embraced or that word love. The need for companionship and wanting to be held through the night is the desire of many people. Having someone there through the tough places in your daily struggle and life's dysfunctions.

Honestly, time is something we can never get back. You can find love again or it will find you. You can lose your money and get on your grind which may motivate a person to obtain money once again. Once time has escaped you, it's gone and the person who you wasted it on as well. Initially, when you meet someone you go in with your own prejudices and expectations. As time passes you project these same thoughts on the other person. We all do this as human beings regardless if it is intentional or not. It happens for the good moments which bring some type of growth and also the negative moments that create distance and issues. How often have you, your friends, family members or loved ones been apart or noticed the death of your relationships. There are plenty of factors that will not allow you to release yourself from the situation. People will not allow themselves to move on from a dead relationship or flatline marriage. Listed below are some key factors that keep people in bondage with themselves and their mates.

1. Sex
2. Children
3. Fear
4. Embarrassment
5. Anger
6. Not wanting another person to be happy
7. Pain
8. Pure Foolishness
9. Being dependent on other people
10. Stubborn
11. Past Experiences
12. Excuses

13. Living a Lie

How long will you stay? These words make people think about their experiences, how they feel about relationships and the time they have invested in their mate. Time and struggles often keep people connected based on their situations together. One thing I can say it is horrible to feel trapped and caged emotionally and mentally in a relationship or situation-ship. So, what do you do? Do you stick it out or do you escape from the madness? How would or have you handled your own personal situations that may have started decaying around you? A bit of advice though, before you decide to encourage someone or be an influence on their decision, make sure you look at your own life. Are you giving them advice from a place of hurt or peace because of what you have endured?

As humanity continues you must understand the words you decide to use are very powerful when you are interacting with your peers, family, and relationships. The Bible speaks of the words you use that speak life or death, along with investing time into the person and being mindful of the company you keep. Friendships, relationships, and marriages are hard work. Every day will not be pleasant or some fairy tale that is portrayed on television and in fictional lover books.

Certain things are needed to make the time you have invested grow like a seed that has been planted. Doing some fairy tale like ideas and actions are very important and beneficial for the nurturing of your friendships and relationships. As we have discussed, having balance is important because it may be the difference of you leaving, staying or being emotionally dead. Being able to discuss the balancing act effect and sticking it out even when it hurst or seems grim. Some may agree or disagree with this or not but true friendships and relationships that last and the ones people value so dearly are the ones that have been tried and tested. For example, some friends and partners will be there when you did not want someone to be there at all. Great relationships and friendships push and motivate you when you are down in the dumps. They do not use it as a moment to attack you. Those type of relationships finds a way to boost you back up when your batteries are low.

The most important thing is not to be a fool as you take things into consideration. The reality of it though is we all have played the fool sometimes in life; some may have experienced it a lot more than others. Don't switch the devil for the witch. The human factor is we switch over what we already have or have experienced because of the newness factor; it's new, fresh, and full of a different kind of fun and energy.

I think people forget there is a honeymoon phase in dating, relationships, and friendships. The honeymoon phase is when a person is giving someone the best representative of themselves to hopefully attract and attach themselves to you. During the honeymoon phase, everything is great, both people are putting effort into their appearance and how they carry themselves especially there grooming. Both are having thoughts about spending time together. The conversations are like have you been here before, have you seen this, would you like to go out, can you come over, how was your day, do you need anything, I enjoyed our conversation, when can I see you again, etc., etc. All of this and much more is the making of a good honeymoon phase.

This point of view is more engaging because you are now developing a new form of intimacy which is called caring. Especially if you are not selfish and think the world is not revolving around you. The honeymoon phase usually stops after six to eight months but depending on the individuals it can be cut short prematurely. It might even last a few extra few months depending on how much people mask their baggage before it starts surfacing.

Poetic Reflections

We use each other

I choose her

But her soul never picked me

In a world of options

She uses me for my time

I use her for what's between her thighs

She Absorb me for my energy

I soak her crazy and denial up like a sponge

I use her for her mind and thoughts that regardless of me she will

always have others

She uses me for my potential hopes, dreams and ambition.

I use her for hustle skills and words she gives to others

I used music

I used basketball

I used the streets

She uses me for motivation and style that hoping it would lead to

the end of the aisle next to somebody Pastor

I use her as my personal project I counsel her through her mental

health

Chapter 11

Things to Remember

The goal is to make everyone a winner even though their thoughts may be in the dumpster. In those moments you can inspire them, or they can decide to just retire and wait to die. You miss the beauty of freedom and a chance to change things, when you no longer feel like you serve a purpose on this blessed surface of trash, garbage, hell and fake prophecies' we call society.

Love is an emotional unpacking of your stuff and not projecting it onto others. Unpacking and releasing often we tend to carry things around with us in our mind, heart, and spirit. As human beings, we have mastered the level of being disappointed and unsatisfied with what we accept or offer to others. For example, some women can go months or years without having sex. They can be disappointed with their partner mentally and sexually and shut themselves down. Women will detach from that feeling, which is natural and healthy, intimacy. Unpacking also means taking that daily mask off people wear daily in life. Don't misunderstand its way beyond the makeup ladies and the beards for gentlemen.

Think of it from this perspective, how long do you allow certain things to rent space in your life? Do you ever outgrow renting? Sometimes life is like an apartment, it serves a purpose for a while. Now as you grow and transcend into different levels, some of us want and need more and want more in love and life. Which is fine and okay, but you must learn to love yourself.

Excuses make you always on the defensive side. Whereas growing and moving create a different place of contentment called peace of mind, which surpasses wealth and money. Become an ambassador and agent of change. When you are standing on the sideline with the sideline complainers, you will not be able to create the type of lifestyle for yourself. All shared experiences are not positive. Sometimes we create our own pain, it's self-inflicting. Our choices, behaviors, actions and decisions can create distance and separation. Remember a person did not just walk out of your life, look at it as God did you a favor and removed them to protect you. Be mindful, some people are just out here trying to pull others into their web of lies.

Contempt talking: Talking down to a person speaking less or not valuing them because of their background or place of origin. You do not agree with their choices and relationships because they do not match up to your core values. You can never love a person or truly care for a person without first respecting them.

Emotional Bullies: People who expect you to give 150% but they do not. Some people will stop loving and dealing with individuals just like they are renting a car. The expectations are for you to give them 150% while they give and tell you what they want you to know. The love they give you is solely based on your actions and efforts you give to them. Before they give you anything, they want to know where you stand in life and where are you in your development of the relationship.

Just because they do not use disrespectful words up, does not mean their words do not mean the same because of their word play usage.

Situational Based Relationships are based on things you give and offer another person, but when that dries out so does the relationship. No disrespect but I have often been told when people in sororities and fraternities stop paying their dues, those relationships do not last much longer. Co-workers are just co-workers for some people; when you stop working at that job how many people still follow up with you check in and on you? Some people may, but there is a clear majority that thinks and feels out sight out of mind.

Notes to take with you and process. You keep learning, striving, growing and improving. This is a never-ending journey of discovering; there is no scoring system. You are the guide of how you choose to learn, love, trust, and focus. The source is healing and not allowing things to steal from your source that is your battery supply. Recharge daily. Do not allow yourself to become empty by life, jobs, friends, family, and bills or anything in life we call responsibilities attached with stress. We must press on and confess on. Less is more. Never be-lieve and trust people who will tell you secrets and gossip about others. It is just a matter of time and chance when your name and character will be coming out of their mouth and lips.

Poetic Reflections

Love is effort

Love is time

Love is work

Love is actions

Love is more than just a word

Love is safety and security

Love creates a space

Love can and will take you to irreplaceable place of sacrifice and

joy

Love will hurt and leave you

Don't mistake love with fear

Chapter 12
Letters to Release & Bury

Often when I'm utilizing counseling theories and performing counseling sessions, there are several methods which can be useful to help an individual heal and move forward with their life when they have been hurt by their past or in a presence moment. It's important to face those issues of concerns and start a rebuilding phase. One method I have used personally and have discussed with individuals to do is a write a letter to a person expressing their concerns and feelings from the past. Letter writing helps to get everything off their mind and heart. I share with them to seal it up, write the address down, place a stamp on it, and release the attachment to the information you wrote down in the letter. Now the key is for you not to mail it but bury it along with those thoughts and feelings. It is a way of letting go and moving forward with your life. The letter releases you to continue to rebuild your life and expectations.

This letter writing is very helpful, but I know it can be kind of foreign now a days with technology. Everyone would rather send a text, send an email and plenty other ways to get there point of views across to other people. This process can be helpful mixed with being therapeutic. It can give you the opportunity to say something or express your feelings and emotions to a person that may no longer be alive, or you are not at a point where you are ready to face someone that hurt you deeply.

Listed below are some letters that I have written for me to move on from some hurtful situations and some other great people that I have met and talked to. They wrote their own letter to be released from their own individual storm because it consumed them for such a long time. Their storms closed them off from love, passion had been sheltered and lost, no attention, depressed, angry, nonchalant, and they became bitter from relationships and falling in love again.

Let me be transparent, I was one those people as I stated earlier in this journey of love in this book. I wanted to be appreciated and loved, but there were other issues I had to deal with; issues that plagued me for years. There are so many people walking around smiling, laughing and displaying great personalities but inside when they are alone, they are crying in the dark. Maybe when you talk to them you talk to their personal wall that they have developed. The wall has become their representative where you may never get to meet the true person because of certain feelings and issues that has captured them. As someone who has endured pain and felt alone, it might be time for you to sit down and be honest with yourself. Pick up a pen and notepad, start writing and coming clean with yourself. Everything you went through or dealing with now you need to take the appropriate steps for you now to bury those thoughts, feelings and emotions forever.

Anthony's Letter

I want you to read this very slowly and understand this is not to-wards you at all. I'm in a different place now with my emotions and for some reason when I try to explain things it comes out wrong. I became the villain, or I immediately get shut down without truly expression the nature of my feelings or any thoughts. What I'm used to is seeing the backside of your head. Meaning watching the back of your head walk out the door when I'm speaking to you and attempting to express things to you. Truly I'm not trying to attack you or make you feel any kind of way about what happen anymore. It happened and it's over with. But it's clear I'm not or was not a good man, boyfriend or just a good friend to be involved with. My emotions are dead, and I have a lot on my plate and my shoulders mixed with other things with in my life that took priority. I did feel like I was in this by myself and I once felt cheated. It's hard to digest things when I only asked for few things which where respect, listening understanding and trust. When I shared my life and the things that tormented me for years I shared with you as a friend and you used it against me when it was convenient. I don't have friends to talk to or express things with, so I confided in you then within in that I had to continue to learn how to deal with things the best way I knew how when you became angry and closed the door on me and my emotions. I'm tired of being judged or having to just suck it up. I feel like I sow into people and what I get in return is bad seeds not a harvest of plenty. So clearly, it's something wrong with me and I how I function and attempt to care and love. In the last two years I have seen my life flip upside down and I have lost a lot of things in that process along with my character, integrity and respect. I also have lost a friend in you that I respected to the core for so many years for so many different reasons. In the process of me losing me and people walking out of my life alcohol became my best friend. When I used to look at my bottles I would smile, and they didn't speak back until you twist the top off and begin to pour. The alcohol is a quit killer depending on how you allow her to love you. Rage and anger began to surface but disappointment and being stagnated arrived internal parking lot which allowed things to fester and bubble up in my world. Even thou I prayed, and I knew it will be brighter days I still laid in my mess. Not blaming a soul but just wanted to hear your voice once more just needed to touch your hand again then I began to drink again. I could not recognize the man in the mirror and when I did recognize him I began to smirk at him because what I witness was not a good looking individual. I would wonder what happen to the real me where did he go then I would tilt my head down because I didn't know I forgot where I left him at. What happens when the liquor bottles, the gym, the interchangeable sexual partners, waking up to different faces does not work anymore. Certain evil thoughts would enter my mind and heart telling me to take my life you have no purpose, nobody wants you. That's why people keep saying the things they do to you walking away from you my tank became more and more empty and I remained lost, but I maintained killing myself in the process trying to hold on but to what I asked myself. I prayed and read my bible and I went to church but by Sunday afternoon or Monday morning I was still was the same back to being the normal dead me inside and outside. I had to learn I was a cracked pot with a hole in it. No matter what a person said to me or how I would attempt to receive the word of God a cracked pot cannot truly receive anything because all the words you get, encouragement and love leaks out it does not have the opportunity to sink into your soul and spirit because it has run out on you. Today I stand and say I'm sorry for hurting you and myself. I know now I hurt so many people with my thoughts, beliefs and stubbornness. I'm sorry for the pain and heartache. I have been told everything happens for a reason and God has to do certain things to get your attention to make you see and know that he is in control not you the individual no matter how much free will a person will develop and have. The God in me is arriving more and more each day as I step back and allow it to come froth and not fight it anymore. The fact that God can change things I will no longer be denied. The Life and destiny that is my birth right I want and need. So, as I ripped off my mask of lies, denial and running away. I have decided to let the past be where it is supposed to be and the way I used to be has died and I buried him along with this letter.

Kima's Letter

Hello to the punk I once loved and believed in. The man I wanted and no one else in my life but you. We were once friends we would talk about everything. I gave you my body and my heart. Then something changed within you. You took my love and tried to control me. Then you hit me because of your wrong doings. The love I had for you turned into fear. For some reason you thought it was your job to control me and instead of loving me. I accepted the abuse joust to have you near, your touch the smell of you that once had turned me on the man I thought I would marry. I had dreams of my father walking me down the aisle to give me away to you. I prayed that you would return to me the real man that I had a great friendship with and the man I loved to life. I prayed that you would return back to the greatness I once saw in you. But all I saw was anger, quietness, pain and mental games. The physical abuse and the mental abuse the words that cut like a blade through my chest. Every day it became more and more some kind of mess. But you would tell me you are sorry then you strike again with your words and heavy hands. The comments, being rude, nasty and hateful. Then you would want to climb on top of me and take my body. I lost my way and my self-esteem was horrible. The tears that would roll down my face. I prayed God I have lost my way and mind. I never have felt this way or ever allowed someone to treat me this way. When I wanted to look in the mirror I would refuse to then when I forced myself to look in the mirror, I saw a face and a body that was empty, and my soul had been depleted. My face bruised eyes red like fire my hair failing out from scalp from all the stress of this hateful relationship.

I felt like a loser. I walked around fronting and lying to keep up an image. An image of pain and hurt but I kept it moving. I did it all working long hours, supporting your goals and dreams which died at the front step of the door. The cooking, cleaning, being sexy and classy at the same time. You did a great job at destroying that side of me hating me because I wanted to improve on myself and life that would have benefited the both of us but that seemed to trouble you. I embraced your insecurities while my passion died by the minute to the moments. Oh, have I cried and died over and over again. It was a long journey and it took a lot of time but today I'm standing thanking God for bringing me through. I no longer blame you completely. I blame myself for loving you and accepting that foolishness. I know I'm better than that. You may never understand but the way I feel and know my steps are ordered. I'm so thankful and beautiful in the same breath. I have the pleasure of loving and being loved. I release you from my soul, spirit, and heart. I prayed for you as well may God Bless you that you become the man God he has placed on this earth to be and not a coward who destroys dreams self-esteem to make himself feel better. As I get on my knees day and night I thank you God for restoring and renewing my mind and heart again. I seal this letter with a caramel kiss to burn and bury those old feelings that you removed from me there is no greater love then you father.

Raymond's Letter

How do I keep you? It's funny when I look at you I see your smile then I think of children and in that instant, I think of the day when we are able to embrace a bundle of joy. God's true earthly blessing of innocents to grow up with a combination of our genes. When I think of leaving something keeps me at home is it because every time I see a smile from you I would melt down. I think of you wandering when that smile will turn into something else and it would cause departure. Departure of outlooks, hopes, dreams, and feelings they all hurt. That smile once it's leaves your face and there is nothing I can offer to bring joy to it. Truly It's not about being insecure, but nothing last forever everything and everyone dies and sprouts out and grows again. Just like the winds blows seeds in different directions and parts of the world its always that chance and opportunity that another can and will cultivate that seed like no other nurturing process that everyone's needs to flourish. I remember how things used to be emotional wise. They were great for you because I was willing to work and give you the world and everything in it. It seems like yesterday but how do you heal a broken heart especially when you try and try but the person you would have died for does not even know the words I love you or the words does not have the same meaning. Pain hurt and frustration through all the bumps and wrong turns not having the forethought to stop and be mindful it really seems like I'm paying for what somebody else has done to you and your family. The one she loved the most who should have had the biggest impression on her life her father. I'm paying for what your father did. Never a real man in her eyes she looked upon me as boy striving to make it and provide. Yes, a boy because she does not have the words of wisdom to even discuss matters like a real caring person instead, she just blows the boy off and tells him nothing pipe down with all that fuzz. Often, I think she wants some old ghetto bull crap and drama coming from a man that gets loud and puts his hands on her and does not come home. Respect, lovemaking, cards, poetry, just because time gifts, poetry from the heart that was giving. There were several obstacles that faced us, but I took them on for us, but she seems not to remember anything. She just made it on her own without support, attention and love. It's like a fight I can't contend for anymore. I must fight for my feelings because I always put other's feelings before mine always have now, I need a little bit of love, inspiration and support and the feeling of being wanted and needed. It's so bizarre because you act like I'm a crack head who has stolen things from you and you look at me like you caught me in your purse taking money when nobody is looking. It's not fair but I keep it moving and I keep so presidential at all times. I wish I could talk to her, laugh with her and play with her especially have a good conversation with her the little special things that don't even cost anything but time and effort. I prayed and asked until I had to vent to others that would listen and die for me. I allowed her and her family to make me feel like I was nothing. I come to realize why it was like that because I'm a good individual who is about to step into their greatness and they wish they could be apart of it. I see you and your family hated on me and disliked and she carried those same feelings into our relationship. I not spiteful I was raised different and built to handle pressure, stress and burdens of others. I'm ready to unload some of my own demons. So, to sum it all up for me I had the best sex of my life last night. I mean some good old lovemaking soul snatching out of this world. There was a lot going on plenty of physical huffing and puffing along with body sweating the feeling of being suspended in time and in the air is priceless. Wow we didn't have the opportunity to make it to the sanctuary better known as the bedroom because when you enter in there and before leaving you will be granted some blessing. I started feeling like Luther if this world was mine. So, something was touched and triggered now and I'm better now and I have found a place to move on much love to you!

Nicole's Letter

I wanted to much with you. You were such a big part of my life and I wanted to always be there. I saw us happy and having a great friendship. I saw a future with you and us having a family someday. All of us going to church and praying together you and me praying together for each other. I saw us growing in the things of God together and working side by side to do what we were called to in the ministry, our children growing up in a home where their parent really loved each other and lived it in front of them. You and I laying in bed at night after our children were sleep talking and laughing about them and planning our family vacations. Every time I thought of this I could only see your face. I believed that you could lead me as you should and later our children to. I saw me becoming a better person because of the man you were. I look at you and see what is in store for you what God has for you. I wanted to take vacations with you have dinner waiting for you every night hold you when it's rough and pray with you be happy with you in times of gladness and encourage you when you can't see how it will work. I could see us driving on a nice day with children in the back because we are so content we just look at each other smile. I didn't just want all these things with you I saw them and that is why my heart is heavy and I'm torn. I know that you will be that man it is already in you. So, when I say you are awesome man of God or a mighty man of God or even that there is a King and greatness in you it's because they are all true and I see them all. You will always be in my heart and I will always love you. I pray God continues to pour his favor out upon you give you uncommon favor with man. I pray that he will direct your footsteps and give unto you the places your feet tread. I pray that your purpose is revealed and the gifts in you are stirred up and that God shows you why you are on the job you work now. I pray all your needs are met. Baby you are my love and I will miss you dearly, but I know the course of events and the direction were set in love then I thought possible it would take shape and form into something great, magical and powerful. I'm sorry for everything continues to walk in the call place upon your life you'll it by the peace it brings.

Jacob's Letter

It was hard when you walked out, left and took the most important thing in my life my baby girl. Through differences, pride, attitudes and emotions that ended the marriage. Spending four years to a lifetime trying to get you to be civil in the process that never will happen. To me the decisions that where made seemed to be planned and calculated one step to the next assisted by your members for the second time. You acted like you was the victim through it all the perfect person who fought for righteousness and stood in the trenches for her family. I never could understand why a person would prevent a man that has been there for you and our child from day one; why would you not allow me to see and build a bond and relationship with our daughter. Just outright preventing and not allowing me to see her. All the lies and games the emotional walls that were placed in my way to block the love I have for her. I missed out on so much time and opportunity to love my baby. Majority of the foolishness based on attitude, control, being stubborn and not being able to see out of your own way or how you would like to say I was not there for you. I'm at fault or the blame because I was out working doing my best to provide of the family unit. You never needed me or my help the fact of feeling and being justified in your doings and the people around you never telling you that the things you are doing is wrong and going along with the wrongness and the mistreatment of another person. The way things where handle still puzzles me to go home to an empty house no furniture just empty walls and empty space. To walk around the house and just see marks all over the walls and muddy food prints stains embedded in the carpet of the house. I never understood how people confess God and sit in church every Sunday and will do wrong to hurt other people because they are hurting and going through something in their life. I learned as a child the difference between Christian and church folk. Trust and believe I'm not perfect but something just doesn't make sense where there are plenty men out here in this world who have children and they do not care about them and do not want to see them or support them. There are men who love their kids and do all they can, and they are prevented by the mother of the kids out of spite or because the relationship ended a certain way. I think about all the traveling up and down the road to see my baby having to take you to court to see my child. Standing up and fighting you and the court system to allow me to be a father so I could just spend time with my child. I think about me going through all the horrible lawyers I had that did not do their job, but they were paid nicely to do nothing. The comments, the attitude and the hatred in seen in your eyes through this process of learning, understanding and letting go. I have had plenty weak moments, but I never lost my mind nor disrespected you even thou you made comments that I did but never saw or heard that one it does come a time in some people life where they just become quiet, stuck with a blank mind set with no comments can come out I guess I was in a state of shocked, depressed and over-whelmed. I would sit there and ask how and why but I learned a long time ago not to question God. I was not perfect, so I dare not point the finger, but a lot of things could have been prevented if I would have begged you to stay like you wanted me to I guess that's something you need from me at the time which refused and did not deliver for you. I guess everything happens for a reason and within in every season there is time for change, time to rebuild, time to let go and move on. I say there are many things sin this world that I once loved and cared for but that does not mean that it is good for me to have them in my life and continue to love on them. Through all of the pain I went through it gave me power a testimony and I'm still standing and fighting, believing and loving.

Jacob's Letter 2

I remember that night like it was yesterday it plays in my mind so vividly. How a lie does not care who tells it and how a stray bullet has no name it just launched out there into the atmosphere to do damage and to harm someone else regardless of its planned or if there is a motive it a sense of not caring or accountability. I have always been aware that there are out there in this world that want to be or get close to you, have you and if that's not possible in the way they see fit it becomes a problem. Some people will take on the mindset of it I can't have I don't want nobody else to have you or I will place my mark on you where I will damage you and burn all bridges to never return. It's amazing how I been told since a child that hell has no fury as a women scorn. The funny thing I have seen it before and witnessed it in other people life the fury and hatred of another person but now I have seen it and witnessed it up close and personally and it actually came knocking at my front door. You never know how strong you will need and must be until certain things happen to you. Now I have some experiences on this subject matter I never wanted to be part of or having any dealings with this particular life lessons on this night when it happens to me. Domesticate lies which the law calls domestic violence. I had to forgive you to save myself I sent out several prayers for you as I remember that night of anger mixed with lies. I recall that day you called me it was your birthday and you was supposed to hang out with your cousins you had this day planned I told you congrats and enjoy your day and that I was working my full-time job and part time. Later that night you called me and told me your plans did not come to pass and could we hang out I remember saying several times no we could not hang out and no we cannot have a drink together. That night you came to my house when you were told not to, but you did anyway banging on my door and windows of the house, because you saw a car at my house. It went from you not listening being upset to straight rage. You were asked several times to leave my resident and your reply was shut fuck up nigga. I need to find out who you have in your house and I need to them how you really are. Still after several prompts and asking you to leave I went to grab my cell phone to call the police I came outside to see you sitting on my front porch sitting Indian style like you was in mediation and I said to you this is my last time asking you to leave if you don't I will call the police. I never forget this statement that change me for a long period of time. You told me you don't want to play that game with me because when they get here I will tell them you beat me. I called the police and stuck my head back into the house. From the inside of my house I watched you move your car out of my drive way I watched you walk over to these college students house outside drinking and smoking talking to them this is when the set up began. I remember six police officers came to the house and two of the police officers chatted with me for about a minute then the other police officers talked to you and the college kids that were outside drinking. I remember asking the officers can you please just make her leave and I will go get a restraining order on Monday morning. I recall one of the police officers just smirking at me like really. I never will forget I'm outside with basketball shorts on, no underwear, no shoes or socks and the police officer walked over to me and asked me to do you have a weapon on me I said no, and they told me to put my hands behind my back and handcuffed me. I got arrested for doing nothing but being at my house when I just got off from my part time job. I remember sitting in the back of the police car asking the officers can I get some shoes, my phone and the keys to lock my house up. You are not going back into the house. The dishearten fact of it all I had witness that the officers never said anything to before the police placed me in back of their car. I asked why and what I'm being arrested for they told me domestic violence. While I sat in the back sit of the police car I could hear you tell the police officer that I beat you and choked you and we lived together and that we have been in a nine-month relationship and that you were eight months pregnant and I was like wow are you serious right now none of what you spoke of was the truth just lies based on anger and immaturity. I think that was one of those times in my life I tucked my head and I became a shame of myself and truly I felt like I hit rock bottom and the feeling of you are truly a loser was hitting me and really consuming me hard, but I kept praying and talking to God. To be hauled off downtown where I used to work at in previous years was so embarrassing and depressing. I sat there in a locked-up room with other people asking me question and questions and I just gave them a look of keep it moving buddy and to hear them say well we will be here until Monday morning. I just kept thinking of my life and little girl and how I was supposed to be at work the next day to do some counseling with my students and parents. The things that kept playing over in my mind were that I'm going to lose my entire career and now I have allowed someone to mess up my name. Through it all I kept praying and talking to God and praying please let me get out of this jail. I need to be at work in the morning. Through the grace of God, I was able to see the magistrate at 3:00am that night and then I had to go through and do some services for pretrial I was released to my sister at 6:00am that Saturday morning where I needed to be at work at 8:00am. The new level of drama that was starting to be released I my life was now just starting when I get home tired mentally drained but so thankful to be free to find that someone broke into my house while I was gone which I already had an ideal of who it was and part of the set up but it was cool I just laugh I was supposed to have been gone for a long extended weekend and not return until Monday morning possibly. The people who did break into my house had a field day and where probably surprised when I returned home so quickly.

Tony's Letter

Where do I begin this letter to my best friend that I met in seventh grade? It's funny how we became close I remember sitting in class and how we would joke on each other and how I built a relationship with your mother who worked at the junior high school that we both went to. The times I used to put you on blast in front of your mother just to get a couple of laughs were priceless at the time. You became more than a friend to me more like a brother to me. I laugh and remember how close we were trying to make those basketball teams and getting cut during try outs then going to play for the recreational leagues and then AAU and doing our thing. I remember all those summers of working out going to basketball camps and just working on our game. I remember when I parents took us to the basketball camp at Campbell University for us to learn the game and become better ball players and students. We both shaved our heads bald for camp it created and a bond and a strong relationship that could never be broken. I remember our times going through high school I played football and started working at a grocery store before you got your job. So, we were not around each other as much we were both about getting paid, but basketball would always bring us back together oh yea plus I forgot we use to burn together. I was not around as much the mix that with two young men trying to find their way in this world and becoming their own man and develop more of an identity for themselves. I remember coming from where we came from you either went away to college or you went into the military, sold drugs, worked at a factory, jail, prison or just did things to speed up death. You had to be fly and your shoe game had to be on point mixed with a swift talk game. I developed my own little crazy style but also acquired somethings and ideas from my brother. I remember our last year run in high school together we did our basketball leagues thing and you went away to North Carolina A&T University. I was still home in the hood not really knowing what I was going to do but I was working and grinding. I was supposed to go to the local community college and get a trade because I played so much in school it was crazy. I ended up at Fayetteville State University well they gave me an opportunity. Then the space between our lives took and went into different directions. The streets were telling me after of couple years had passed by you were not in school anymore and you went way to school in Florida for a trade and then you came back to our county military town. Then you got in some trouble with the law and you were doing some community service in the hood and that is when I saw you and we reconnected again. My brother life had changed going through the ups and down of his own life and not having positive males around him. I was so caught up in me and developing me with working two jobs and going to school and running the streets as doing my own thing I forgot about my best friend, my brother that I knew since seventh grade. I never had the chance to take you to be around some more positive brothers that we all grew up with that moved away to start their lives and better themselves. We embraced each other, and it allowed all of us to experience many different things but with the grace of God we made I through all those experiences and it allowed us to grow up and become good men. But I forgot about my brother so consume with me and what I was doing that I lost you but never ever forgot about you. I remember stopping by your mother house to come see you and she told me I just had missed you that you went walking to somebody house to hang out. My intention was for me to take you somewhere, so we could and make some moves like we used to and get away from our old stomping grounds, but I never show you again. It has been many years ago, but I remember it like yesterday my brother Vince found out that you had died, and he kept calling me that day and I would not answer my phone because I was working with a client and then Vince called my mother and told her and she said she had just found out and she wanted to be the one to tell me. I couldn't believe it I was like no way not possible and mother showed me the story in the Fayetteville Observer it was like my heart dropped for a little while and then tears started to form in my eye for my brother that I felt I could have helped save but my time our time had escaped us. I don't think it registered to me until I went to your mother house and I saw her face and the family face your mother was strong brother. I walked in your room and remembered all the great times we had talking trash, talking about girls, how fly and fresh we dressed, and our game was I admit you had me with the school game for a little while you used to kill them and then most importantly discussing our future. Man, I miss you we never got a chance to experience life together as adults with our families our old friends and new friends. My brother Charles I was blessed with a beautiful little girl that I know you see from the heavens about and smile down on her, but I wish you had the opportunity to play with her and talk to her like my other family and bothers do from time to time. The day of the funereal I never knew how strong your mother was at the time I have seen and witness certain things over the years as we were growing up. Your mother didn't take any junk, but she was always cool, calm and collective. I know how much she loved you. You were a momma's boy and so was I. That day I could never forget your mother made sure I was beside her at all times and insisted that I rode in the limousine with her she told me I want to say something about you I know how close you guys where and I replied with my country respectable yes momma. In that Limousine I wrote you a poem talking about you and how I remembered the real you not what everybody may have saw once life experiences and self-inflicting behaviors crossed our paths but I could barley get through it when I was called up to speak and it was so much more I should have said but things I should have said did not come out I just had a raspy voice and a couple of tears. Many people had their own thoughts and opinions based on how you changed but they would always keep it respectable when I was around because of the respect level they have for me and the relationship and bond we had as kids. I know and have been blessed to be around a good brother with a good heart that may have lost his way but did not have the opportunity to completely come back to his real self and bless people with his God giving talents. I love you black man always! I still pour out liquor for you I love brother.

Lisa's Letter

Wow we started this whole thing off bad and never really got a chance to build anything. As much as I remember and will never forget that day neither will ever fade away in my mind. I just remember being so excited to come over and when I got there just feeling so comfortable. But my being comfortable got buried and interrupted by stupidity and while I'm sitting there in your place all alone in the darkness while you were outside entertaining that dumb hussy and then unfortunately you are being placed in handcuffs. I'm asking myself what I got* myself into what did I get myself into what did I walk into. This man is just like everybody else out here playing games with females' minds. Taking a long drive back home when my mind and just thinking and going through the motion of I really like this guy, but I must keep him at a distance, so I won't get hurt and don't get serious because obviously he has whole a lot of stuff going on with already. So, with that on my mind and me convincing myself not to get to involved with you I then brought myself right back over the next day not to talk and get to know you better and ask questions about the life you live but to have drunk sex. Damn we started off so wrong and set ourselves up to fail. It was so much against us from day one. All the negative things and thoughts I had, you made me the happiest I had been in awhile you made me laugh, smile forget the hurt and pain feel as if I had a purpose and reason to be here to have met you but still in the back of my mind and weighting heavy on my heart was that I'm not ready and I'm scared as hell to give you my all and maybe just maybe these feelings and you were just to good to be true so I continued to keep you at a distance but still allowing my heart to fall for you, it's crazy I know but that's how it happened. Because I was so selfish and caught up in my ways of thinking and not wanting you to know that I was starting to care for you. I ended up hurting you by my words I didn't mean because I thought I had to keep you at this distance so that you couldn't hurt or play with my heart only to realize I was hurting you. I really messed up and we started off so wrong and never gave ourselves an opportunity to really have or even build a friendship all we had was sex always bringing us back together and at the same time always tearing us apart. We knew we should have stopped this a long time ago but something other than sex was keeping us in each other life. I love you more then you know or believe, and I want you to know you will always have this huge place in my heart forever! I guess and know this is bye for us now I pray not forever but I know I will always have love for you.

Christian's Letter

   As I sit in this chair, I look at what I have on this table and what sit before me a gun, my bible a bottle of whiskey and couple of joints. Where do I go and stand? I know my life has become a pathway of trash and garbage. I'm so alone I hear people say pray, pray and pray some more but God he hasn't heard my cry and if he has, he is not responding to me. My heart and mind is in so much turmoil. The feelings I have is that I want to die why am I here. Forget this purpose crap people keep speaking of. I have tried, I gave, I fought a good fight I believe I have giving all I can, and I still lose, and I'm truly lost. Thoughts of killing myself I have consumed me more and more. Nobody gets me or know my heart and the passion I give, and I kept just a little for me and know I feel kike the enemy. The enemy of myself. As I drink this whiskey and I enter bullets into my gun. I feel somewhat justified you fight and friend and work hard to have things and love of people with proper perspective. I played the game by the book or I did it the so-called right way, but I have not prospered I still see the dead end and face the road-blocks my life has been under construction for a long time now. So, I send this letter to all I have loved and who have loved me. I do realize this a selfish move that I'm making, and I will not see God's glory but I'm ready to go. I can't make it here in this world and life. To all I leave behind you will forget me soon and call me a fool or weird. Yes, I agree slightly a little bit different or unique. To the kids, adults or people in general I have spoken to or tried to influence that was all from God and you helped me more than I ever helped you I thank you. To my family and friends, I'm truly sorry more ways than one and in another perspective it's what needed to be done for me to keep me in your hearts. I never made my legacy but take my memoirs where I can land, and I hope I can see you and look at all the greatness that you guys have developed and acquired for yourselves. Well I shared no more tears over myself no more attitudes from people. A letter from a real man turned coward! Maybe God will forgive me since he knew my heart from the very start. Goodbye!